Teachings of the Sikh Gurus

The Sikh Gurus comprise a unique lineage of ten spiritual masters, beginning with Guru Nanak (b. 1469) and ending with the enigmatic warrior-saint Guru Gobind Singh (d. 1708). The Gurus passed on their teachings of equality and brotherhood through several thousand poems and hymns of surpassing beauty and directness, which are enshrined in the two key scriptures of the Sikh religion, the Adi Granth and the Dasam Granth, both recognized masterpieces of Indian literature. The Adi Granth in particular is so important in Sikhism that it takes centre stage in the physical layout of all temples and in ceremonies of worship. Possessing a unique status marked by its honorific title of Guru Granth Sahib, it is both hymnal and prayer book as well as an infallible reference text. Because of its remarkable influence, Sikhism is often described as a 'religion of the book'.

Teachings of the Sikh Gurus presents a brand new selection of key highlights from the Guru Granth Sahib and Dasam Granth, translated into modern English by two leading experts. Thematically organized by topics such as Time and Impermanence, Self and Mind, Ethical Being, Authority and Knowledge, the book's accessible and carefully chosen extracts distil the essence of Sikhism's remarkable textual and intellectual legacy, showing how its message of universal tolerance suits the contemporary world. Complete with a detailed introduction, these lively and accurate translations are an essential resource for Sikhs and students of Sikhism.

Teachings of the Sikh Gurus

Selections from the Sikh Scriptures

Edited and translated by
Christopher Shackle
and
Arvind-pal Singh Mandair

Routledge
Taylor & Francis Group

LONDON AND NEW YORK

First published 2005 by Routledge
2 Park Square, Milton Park, Abingdon, Oxon OX14 4RN

Simultaneously published in the USA and Canada
by Routledge
711 Third Avenue, New York, NY 10017

Routledge is an imprint of the Taylor & Francis Group, an informa business

© 2005 Christopher Shackle and Arvind-pal Singh Mandair

Typeset in Joanna by RefineCatch Limited, Bungay, Suffolk

All rights reserved. No part of this book may be reprinted
or reproduced or utilized in any form or by any electronic,
mechanical, or other means, now known or hereafter
invented, including photocopying and recording, or in
any information storage or retrieval system, without
permission in writing from the publishers.

British Library Cataloguing in Publication Data
A catalogue record for this book is available from the British Library

Library of Congress Cataloging in Publication Data
Shackle, C.
   Teachings of the Sikh Gurus : selections from the Scriptures / Christopher
Shackle and Arvind-pal Singh Mandair.—1st ed.
     p. cm
     1. Sikh gurus. 2. Nåanak, Guru, 1469–1538. 3. Sikhism—Doctrines.
I. Mandair, Arvind-pal Singh. II. Title.
     BL2018.5.G85S46 2005
     294.6′82—dc22   2004024960

ISBN 13: 978-0-415-26603-1 (hbk)
ISBN 13: 978-0-415-26604-8 (pbk)

CONTENTS

ACKNOWLEDGEMENTS

This book has taken much longer to complete than was originally envisaged either by ourselves or by our publishers. We must particularly acknowledge John Hinnells as our steady Alpha et Omega, who several years ago was the spur for its initial conception and who recently so graciously assisted at its final delivery. After taxing the patience of several previous editors through our postponements of earlier deadlines, we are grateful to the current Routledge team of Lesley Riddle and Gemma Dunn for their enthusiastic support in achieving its attractive published form, which has been much enhanced by Jeevan Deol's suggestion of the painting of Guru Nanak which adorns its cover.

CHRISTOPHER SHACKLE
ARVIND-PAL SINGH MANDAIR
JANUARY 2005

INTRODUCTION

0.1 The Sikh Gurus and the Sikh Scriptures

0.1.1 Devotional Traditions in Mughal India

The richness and variety of India's religious literatures have long been recognized in the West. Until recently, though, Western attention has focused primarily on the earliest texts composed before the Christian era, like the Vedas and other core texts of the Hindu tradition composed in Sanskrit, or the Dhammapada and other foundation texts of Buddhism recorded in Pali. While the significance of these early literatures has thus long been widely recognized, many more recent religious texts of major importance composed in India over the last millennium in early forms of the modern languages descended from Sanskrit have been relatively neglected, even though they often enjoy far greater living currency in South Asia today than the Sanskrit religious literature.

Many of these texts date from the very fertile period of the Mughal empire, the last of the great Indian empires of the pre-colonial era, which controlled northern India for most of the sixteenth and seventeenth centuries. As a result of the major presence of Islam in the region, which had been established by earlier Muslim conquests, Indian society was one of great religious and cultural diversity. Defined at its extremes by the Islam of the clerics and the Hinduism of the Brahmins with their ritualistic emphases, the religious life of the period found much of its most vibrant expression in several overlapping currents of devotional poetry. Reflecting an upsurge of religious awareness on either side of the formal Muslim–Hindu divide, these currents were inspired on the one hand by Sufism with its emphasis upon a loving inward experience of the divine, on the other by the Hindu tradition known as *sagun bhakti*, the devotion to a particular manifestation of the divine, especially to Krishna and to Ram as incarnations of Vishnu. The broad appeal of both was reflected in the variety of literary expression which each inspired, ranging from texts written in Persian and in Sanskrit, the elite languages of the day, to more popular compositions in the local languages of northern India which were at that time otherwise little used for writing.

Besides these two major devotional traditions, there was also a third which went rather further than either in the pursuit of a devotional ideal detached from established orthodoxy. This is the tradition known as *nirgun bhakti*, devotion to the divine unqualified by attributes, which is associated with a number of loosely linked teachers generically referred to as the Sants or 'saints'. Typically without the links to elite culture characteristic of both Sufis and devotees of Krishna, the Sants relied exclusively on verses and hymns written in a popular style in the local languages to get their message across. The most memorable of this Sant poetry is that composed by the great fifteenth-century teacher Kabir of Benares, the author of most of the best-remembered verses of all medieval Hindi poetry.

Of the many new religious movements which arose in Mughal India, it is the Sikhs of the Punjab who have most successfully established a distinct religious identity both originally in India and now throughout much of the world. So while in a general mapping of these movements, the teachings of Guru Nanak (1469–1539) are certainly aligned with the 'third way' of *nirgun bhakti*, Sikh tradition rightly insists on the originality of the inspiration of the first of the Sikh Gurus.

The representative anthology of fresh translations presented in this volume is intended to open ways to understanding something of the range and power of the teachings of Guru Nanak and his successors, who constitute the unique lineage of spiritual masters which culminates with the warrior-saint Guru Gobind Singh (1666–1708). Their teachings are contained in the Sikh scriptures, the two massive collections known respectively as the Adi Granth or Guru Granth Sahib, and the Dasam Granth.

The following sections of this opening part of our introduction describe the evolution of the Guruship and the Sikh scriptural tradition. The central part of the introduction then looks in more detail at the actual teachings of the Sikh Gurus, with attention first to the typical forms of their expression, then to the main themes of their content, and finally to how modern understandings of them have been shaped by the processes of commentary and translation initiated in the colonial period. Against this necessary context, the concluding part of our introduction is then directed more specifically at the contents of this volume, as we explain its arrangement and rationale, and say something about the principles which have governed our strategy of translation.

Rather than encumbering the text of the introduction with bibliographic references to the relevant literature, we have thought it preferable to consolidate our bibliography at the end of the volume. This is arranged to follow the layout of the introduction, to enable readers to follow up areas of particular interest to them.

0.1.2 The Sikh Gurus

The Sikh scriptures are almost exclusively concerned with the devotional message of the Gurus' teachings, so understandings of the Gurus' lives are largely dependent upon non-scriptural hagiographies composed by later Sikh authors and the occasional testimony of independent sources. The special importance of Guru Nanak as the first Guru is reflected in the substantial body of hagiographical literature contained in the *janamsakhis* or 'life testimonies', which emerged over a century and a half after Nanak and underwent further expansion until printed versions appeared in the nineteenth century.

According to what has become the most influential of these narratives, the *Puratan Janamsakhi*, Nanak was born in Talwandi, a village 65 kilometres west of Lahore in the Punjab, into a family of the Khatri caste specializing in business and record-keeping. Although he was professionally trained, unlike such Sant teachers as the weaver Kabir, Nanak is said always to have shown far greater interest in religion, and although diligent in his duties as an administrator for a local Muslim nobleman in the town of Sultanpur, he remained mainly preoccupied in spiritual matters, preferring to discourse with holy men and wandering ascetics about the meaning of life. His closest associate was Mardana, a Muslim bard from his home village. Together at Sultanpur, Nanak and Mardana organized nightly performances of devotional songs, going to bathe in a nearby river at daybreak. It was during one of these morning baths that Nanak, then aged thirty, underwent a powerful mystical experience, in which he received a divine calling to bring people to an awareness of God's Name.

Presumed to have drowned after a three-day absence, Nanak returned from the river seemingly unharmed but maintained a silence punctured only by responding to all questions with the uncanny reply: 'There is no Hindu, there is no Muslim' (na ko hindu, na ko musalman). Although nowhere recorded in the scriptures, this statement not only gave a glimpse of the political implications of Nanak's religious experience vis-à-vis the idea of a religiosity beyond social and cultural boundaries, but also indicated the futility of a way of thinking based on the construction of the 'other' in opposition to the 'self'. Exemplified in his own day by the tendency to define oneself as 'Hindu' in opposition to 'Muslim' and vice versa, the process of 'othering' was fundamentally opposed to Nanak's understanding of Oneness.

For the next twenty years, according to the Puratan Janamsakhi, Guru Nanak travelled extensively taking his message to the four corners of the Indian subcontinent and beyond. Just before the first Mughal emperor Babur began his successful conquest of India in 1526, Guru Nanak at the age of fifty founded a small commune at Kartarpur near Lahore, where he settled down to lead a small circle of his Sikhs or 'disciples'. There they were instructed to live their lives according to a routine that included cleansing of one's body by daily bathing, cleansing of the mind through meditation on the Name, the regular singing of devotional hymns, the pursuance of a healthy work ethic and the maintenance of a regular family life.

Among his followers was a devotee called Lahina, whom Nanak renamed as his 'limb' Angad and later designated as his successor, so that he became the second Guru of the Sikhs until his death in 1552. This step marked the start of the consolidation of the early Sikh community through a succession of living Gurus, whose powers of organization were one of the reasons that the Nanak-panth or path stemming from Nanak proved to be so much more successful than the looser movements deriving from other Sants, like the Kabirpanth. During the time of the third Guru Amar Das (1552–74), this formal organization of the community was first realized with the appointment of local leaders responsible to the Guru's headquarters at Goindval on the banks of the river Beas.

All the Sikh Gurus were members of the Khatri caste, and after the fourth Guru Ram Das (1574–81) the Gurus were all drawn from the same family. Since there was no rule of primogeniture, the succession to the Guruship regularly provoked disputes and the breakaway of sectarian groups around disappointed candidates. Thus the fifth Guru Arjan (1581–1606) had to face particularly vigorous opposition from his elder brother Prithi Chand, and trad-ition depicts this as being one of the motivating factors behind the important organizational measures which the Guru undertook. Guru Arjan made two very significant contributions to the consoli-dation of the early Sikh community. One was to give it an enduring central text, the Adi Granth or 'Original Scripture', which as a formal creation was perhaps in part inspired by the dominant Mus-lim ideology of a scripture as the chief mark of an authentic religious community. The other was to provide it with a permanent central location, the great temple of the Harimandir, the so-called 'Golden Temple', located at Amritsar, the centre first established by his father Guru Ram Das which was over the centuries to become the prime sacred site of Sikhism. The ceremonial installation in the new temple in 1604 of the new scripture, containing the composi-tions of all the first five Gurus, marked the apogee of the first phase of the era of the Guruship.

The growing strength of the Sikh community and of Guru Arjan's personal influence in the region, which was strategically situated at a sensitive point on the main route between the most important cities of the Mughal empire, was however also gained at the always risky price of involvement in imperial affairs. When the usual war of succession followed the death of the famously tolerant emperor Akbar in 1605, Guru Arjan was charged with having supported an unsuccessful candidate for the throne and was consequently executed on the orders of the new emperor Jahangir, thus initiating a long and proud tradition of Sikh martyrdom for the faith.

This involvement with the Mughal authorities persisted throughout the seventeenth century under the later Gurus. The sixth Guru Hargobind (1606–44) consciously prepared the Sikhs to resist state oppression through military means as and when this became necessary. During the tenure of Guru Hargobind's successors the seventh Guru Har Rai (1644–61) and the eighth Guru Har Krishan (1661–4) overt confrontation largely receded. None of these three Gurus composed hymns which found a place in the scriptures. The next recognized contributor to the scriptures is the ninth Guru Tegh Bahadur (1664–75), who was again forced to confront the increasingly hostile religious policies of the last great Mughal emperor Aurangzeb (1658–1707). Guru Tegh Bahadur's active resistance to these policies led to his imprisonment and his public execution in the Chandni Chowk in the centre of Delhi, where the site of his martyrdom is celebrated by a famous Sikh temple.

The preceding Gurus' strategies of resistance culminated in the life and work of the tenth and last Sikh Guru Gobind Singh (1666–1708). Proclaiming an ambitiously renewed mission, Guru Gobind Singh undertook the wholesale reorganization of the Sikhs with the creation of the militant brotherhood of the Khalsa, a body of warriors personally dedicated to the Guru, outwardly defined by the uncut hair and other symbols of the observant adult male Sikh. The new religio-political order of the Khalsa was designed not only to give a practical shape to Guru Nanak's ideal of the guru-guided life but also to defend the Sikhs in the face of increasingly aggressive imperial policies. Much of Guru Gobind Singh's life was occupied in armed struggle with the forces of the emperor Aurangzeb's officers and local allies. During these wars, all four of the Guru's sons were killed, and the line of living Gurus came to an end with Guru Gobind Singh's death in 1708.

While the large body of writings associated with Guru Gobind Singh himself was collected in a new scripture called the Dasam Granth or 'Scripture of the Tenth One', the Guruship itself was transferred in a unique development after the tenth Guru's death to the eternal Word enshrined in the scripture of the Adi Granth, now expanded by the inclusion of Guru Tegh Bahadur's hymns. This was an act rich in religious and political implications, since the *bani* or Word of the scriptural text, which received the honorific title of Guru Granth Sahib, was now to be acknowledged as the basis for religious and temporal authority as well as the medium of spiritual knowledge. Sikhs were to live their lives in response to it and it was to be central to all that happened in Sikh life.

Quite without real parallel in other Indian religions, the immense importance of the Guru Granth Sahib is most obviously manifested in the central place given to the scripture in the physical layout of a Sikh temple or gurdwara. While it is in no sense a book containing the sort of laws and rules characteristic of the Semitic scriptures, the Guru Granth Sahib, as a hymnal and prayer book and as the focus of private, congregational and communal devotion, naturally dictates much of the liturgy. It also provides the text of the unbroken readings of the entire scripture (*akhand path*) by teams of readers, which are so popular a ritual in modern Sikhism, not to speak of its role as an infallible reference text, whether for counsel in times of difficulty or as a help in determining the name to be given a newborn child. Sikhism is thus, in a sense that is peculiar to its tradition, a 'religion of the book' and is hardly to be understood without an appropriate understanding of its scripture.

0.1.3 The Sikh Scriptures

The status of the Adi Granth as the primary scripture of the Sikhs is thus a very special one, and so too is the character of its contents and organization. In its modern form, which dates from after the introduction of printing to the Punjab in the nineteenth century, it has a standard format of 1,430 pages. It is printed in the Gurmukhi script, believed to have been developed by the second Guru Angad, which has always been used as the principal medium for writing most Sikh religious literature, and which is nowadays the standard script for writing Punjabi in India. The text is printed in continuous lines, with breaks only for major new sections.

Structurally the Adi Granth is composed of three main sections of very unequal length. The first is a brief liturgical section (pp. 1–13) containing works that a devout Sikh will recite or sing each day: the *Japji* by Guru Nanak which is prescribed for recitation in the early morning hours, and the hymns by the Gurus prescribed for the evening prayer (*Rahiras*) and the night prayer (*Sohila*). The somewhat longer final section (pp. 1353–1430) contains collections of shorter verses by the Gurus and others, along with poems of praise in honour of the Gurus composed by their court poets, the Bhatts or 'Bards'.

The main body of the scripture (pp. 14–1353) is a vast collection of hymns, whose primary arrangement is by the raga in which they are to be performed. Within the primary category of the thirty-one main ragas which are distinguished as separate headings, the hymns of the Gurus are next organized by their poetic form, beginning with the shortest, which may occupy only a few lines of text, and gradually progressing to much longer compositions, which may each take up several pages. It is within these formal categories that authorship is finally distinguished, beginning with the hymns of Guru Nanak, followed by those of the other Gurus in chronological order. Since all the Gurus used the same poetic signature 'Nanak', their compositions are distinguished by the code-word *Mahala*, abbreviated as M, so that the hymns of Guru Nanak himself are labelled as M1, those of the third Guru Amar Das as M3, and so on. After the hymns of the Gurus, most ragas then conclude with shorter groups of hymns of *nirgun bhakti* inspiration by non-Sikh poets of the pre-Guru period, like Kabir, Namdev and Ravidas. These authors are generically known as the Bhagats or 'Saints'.

In all, the Adi Granth contains some 6,000 separate compositions. As has already been explained, these are of uneven length, but an approximate idea of the proportional representation of the main contributors may be gained from counting the numbers of hymns and verses attributed to them. Of the Sikh Gurus whose works are included in the scripture, Guru Nanak has 974 compositions, Guru Angad 62, Guru Amar Das, 907, Guru Ram Das 679, Guru Arjan 2,218, and Guru Tegh Bahadur 116. Of the non-Sikh Bhagats much the greatest number of compositions are attributed to Kabir with 541, although many of these are very short verses. These statistics need of course to be understood in the light of the qualitatively central importance of Guru Nanak's own profoundly comprehensive and original contribution, which acted as the primary inspiration of all his successors.

In the formation of the scripture as a whole, the key figure is

Guru Arjan, himself much the largest contributor to the Adi Granth, which as a collection stands as striking testimony to his skill as its chief redactor. As is the case with many other scriptures, the traditional story of the creation of the Adi Granth tells how it came into being through divine inspiration, in this case channelled through the Guru as he produced the canonical text in one sustained effort with the aid of Bhai Gurdas, his chief disciple and amanuensis. In recent years, however, the formation of the canon has become the subject of scholarly studies, which have begun to use the manuscript evidence to show that the process was a more complex one, which certainly extended over a considerably longer period than is envisaged in the traditional account. Much scholarly work still remains to be done on the historical formation and textual history of the Adi Granth and its contents, as well as of the quite extensive apocryphal material attributed to the Gurus but excluded from the scripture.

The canonical status of the Adi Granth as an authentic record of the teachings of the Sikh Gurus nevertheless remains unquestioned, with differences of opinion being voiced only as to its final item (pp. 1429–30), a list of ragas which does not correspond to those used in the primary arrangement of the scripture itself. In contrast to this universal acceptance, there is a much lesser degree of consensus among the Sikh community when it comes to the other book of scripture, the Dasam Granth which is associated with the tenth Guru Gobind Singh.

The appearance of modern printed editions of the Dasam Granth, with their 1,428 pages of Gurmukhi type, are certainly planned to look as similar as possible to those of the Adi Granth. But this is a very different kind of book. In place of the skilful arrangement of hymns by different authors within the Adi Granth, the Dasam Granth consists of a miscellany of different items, many of which do not seem to be placed in any particularly logical order, and few of which are unambiguously marked as the work of the Tenth Master himself (*Patshahi* 10). Its original compilation is supposed to have been undertaken in the early eighteenth century by Guru Gobind Singh's close disciple Bhai Mani Singh, but once again the manuscript evidence suggests that the collection and eventual finalization of its contents was a more gradual process.

The Dasam Granth enjoyed considerable scriptural authority in the eighteenth and early nineteenth centuries as the authentic work of the tenth Guru. During this period, the religious and political affairs of the Sikhs were dominated by forces of the militant Khalsa founded by Guru Gobind Singh. These forces moved successfully from armed resistance to the declining Mughal empire towards the creation of an independent kingdom of the Punjab under Maharaja Ranjit Singh (1799–1839). But the status of the Dasam Granth began to be challenged when, following the British conquest of the region in the 1840s, the reformist Singh Sabha movement emerged in the later nineteenth century. This led to the successful redefinition of Sikhism as an ethical monotheism which was to be seen, on the basis of the teachings of the Sikh Gurus as contained in the Adi Granth, as being quite distinct from Hinduism.

Much of the Dasam Granth proved difficult to accommodate within the reformist scheme, since by far the largest part of its contents are devoted either to lengthy poetic reworkings from Puranic sources of what was now seen to be distinctively Hindu mythology, or else to a vast collection of 'Tales of Deceit' (Charitropakhyan) from a whole variety of sources, which appeared to be distinctively secular rather than spiritual in inspiration. By contrast, devotional hymns of the kind which comprise most of the Adi Granth are very few in number in the Dasam Granth. The modern tendency has therefore been to reserve canonical status for only those hymns and autobiographical poems, collectively making up only a relatively small proportion of the whole Dasam Granth, which can be safely attributed to Guru Gobind Singh himself as being compatible with a modern Sikh definition of scripture which is based primarily upon the supremely authoritative Adi Granth as Guru Granth Sahib.

0.2 The Teachings of the Sikh Gurus

0.2.1 Form

The teachings of the Gurus are not cast as philosophical treatises or as legal codes to be silently read, but as poetry with a strongly devotional emphasis, which is designed to be sung or recited. As one of India's great religious poets, Guru Nanak's spiritual insightfulness is fully matched by his poetic skill, and his carefully inspired union of form with content sets the pattern for all his successors until fresh approaches are developed in Guru Gobind Singh's works. Many of the formal features of the Gurus' hymns cannot be precisely conveyed in modern English translation (a point to which we return at the end of this introduction in section 0.3.3 below), and it is therefore important here to preface a summary of their teachings with an overall description of the medium in which they are so significantly cast.

While the Gurmukhi script uniformly used for writing the Sikh scriptures is a graphic badge of their common religious affiliation, the language of their contents is considerably more varied than the simplistic modern equation of the Gurmukhi script with the Punjabi language can too easily suggest. Just as India is a highly multi-lingual country today, in which English, Hindi and the many regional languages and dialects operate in different contexts along-side one another, so too were many languages used for different purposes in the Mughal period, when Persian was the language of administration and courtly poetry, and Sanskrit the learned medium of Brahminic culture.

The modern Indo-Aryan languages like Punjabi and Hindi, which are descended from Sanskrit, form a quite closely related family comparable to the Romance languages descended from Latin. Since India has historically lacked strong nation-states of the European type within which Spanish, French or Italian became sharply differentiated from one another, the literary evolution of particular languages was here more typically tied to religious movements. The most prominent north Indian poetic language of the period was the Braj Bhasha of the region near Agra particularly associated with Krishna, which was used for the creation of a sophisticated tradition of *sagun bhakti* devotional poetry by Guru Nanak's near contemporary, the Brahmin Surdas, and his many successors.

The lower caste Sant teacher-poets, like the weaver Kabir or the leather-worker Ravidas, were hardly concerned with the sort of poetic sophistication associated with the Brahminic class whose authority they so expressly challenged. In order to spread their message by the most direct means, their verse accordingly incorporates a variety of regional forms but tends to be based on the Old Hindi of the Delhi region which was likely to be more widely understood than other more localized dialects. Surpassing them all in the frequent subtlety of his linguistic choices, including the use of dialect forms as well as of frequent loanwords from Sanskrit and Persian, Guru Nanak combined this poetic language of the Sants with his native Old Punjabi. It is this mixture of Old Punjabi and Old Hindi which constitutes the core idiom of all the earlier Gurus.

While this 'sacred language of the Sikhs' remains broadly intelligible to speakers of modern Punjabi, the linguistic changes that have taken place over the intervening centuries mean that its careful understanding is dependent upon some special study. In particular, the scriptural language is much more highly inflected than modern Punjabi, but many of the case endings on which the precise meaning often depends have been lost by phonetic changes. The modern reading pronunciation of the Gurmukhi text consequently disregards the many short vowels written at the end of words, so that written *gharu* 'house', *ghara* 'houses', *ghari* 'in the house' are all pronounced as *ghar*, a practice which tends to blur the sense of the often highly condensed expression favoured by Guru Nanak in particular.

In keeping with the progressive move of the developing Guruship into the cultural mainstream, the language of the scripture gradually shows an increased proportion of Braj Bhasha forms and of learned Sanskritic vocabulary. This tendency is certainly apparent in the hymns of Guru Arjan, whose great quantity also provides fascinating evidence of the encyclopaedic linguistic sophistication with which he used virtually all the literary idioms of his time as part of the universalistic construction represented by the vast scripture to whose size he himself made so massive a contribution. This movement from local idiom to sophisticated literary language is finally completed by the time of the ninth Guru Tegh Bahadur, whose hymns are composed in Braj Bhasha. The linguistic profile of the Dasam Granth, too, shows it to be the conscious product of a Guruship whose power had assumed all the trappings of an established court. Braj Bhasha is the dominant language of most of its contents, along with the creative employment of freely coined new vocabulary, while its final pages contain items composed in Persian, the Mughal court language, though printed in the Gurmukhi not the Arabic script.

The conscious choices made available to the Gurus by the considerable variety of the linguistic media available to them are important for understanding the stylistic implications of individual compositions, and something is said about these in the short introductions to the sections in which our translations are grouped. An even greater, if even less translatable, role is played by the musical settings of their hymns. The Sikh Gurus were well versed in contemporary styles of Indian music. For example, popular depictions of Guru Nanak (as on the cover of this book) show that his constant companion Mardana was a trained musician specializing in the stringed instrument called *rabab* or rebeck. Guru Nanak and his successors wished their hymns to be sung to ragas that expressed the emotions of the text, and the performance style to be compatible with the meaning of the hymn.

The role of the ragas is therefore not supplementary to the text, as is often thought, but central, as according to Indian aesthetic theory each musical raga evokes and expresses a definite mood that has its own distinctive flavour (*rasa*), which may vary across a spectrum that ranges from adoration and rejoicing to desolation and entreaty. To render the raga correctly in performance (*kirtan*) is to correctly express one particular mood and not another. In order to reproduce a certain mood, traditions of Sikh musicology (*gurmat sangit*) stress the performance rules and melodic material as the best way of maintaining the individual properties of a raga and of preserving the broad message of a particular hymn. Each hymn is therefore set to a pre-defined raga, and when it is sung the nature and feelings associated with this raga affect the lyrical interpretation of the text. Sikh music thus has some limitation placed on it so that the spiritual aspect of the performance can be maintained. In performance, therefore, the purpose of setting the Guru's words to a raga is to make an impression on the ego or self-conscious aspect of the listener's mind in such a way that it is forced into dialogue with its unconscious aspect, the heart or soul. When these two different aspects of the mind speak to each other, it is said to be attuned with its divine ground. The Gurus aimed to convey experience through feelings and moods because they make up an aspect of consciousness which cannot be reduced to conceptuality, and it is always important to remember the significance of this lyrical dimension when approaching the record of the Gurus' teachings which is contained in the text of their hymns as they appear, silently, on the printed page.

All the compositions of the Gurus are in verse. At the most general level, their verse can be defined by certain common characteristics, shared with most medieval Indian poetry, which have important implications of their own for understanding the Gurus' message. It is composed in short units, with the end of each line being marked by a strong rhyme, and with longer lines generally being broken by a marked caesura. Since there is no grammatical run-on from line to line, each self-contained syntactic unit has to be quite short, thus favouring a typically condensed and direct style of expression which relies on such devices as parallelism and varied repetition for its cumulative effects. Like other nirgun bhakti poets, the earlier Gurus do not allow themselves to be too strictly bound by the exact metrical rules of Hindi poetics, and individual lines or half-lines are often expanded by a word or phrase which is additional to the strict metrical count.

This feature is particularly common in the case of the author's signature (chhap) which is a standard mark of closure in all Indian poetic genres. As already explained, all the Gurus (except for Guru Gobind Singh, whose compositions are normally unsigned) use the same signature 'Nanak', typically as a vocative self-address in the sense of 'O Nanak', or more explicitly spelt out as 'Nanak says'. Formally, the poetic genres so marked by the Gurus' signature are very varied, including many of common medieval Indian types, others directly inspired by Punjabi folk forms, and some which are invented as unique creations. Four main categories of poetic form may be distinguished.

The bulk of the Adi Granth is made up of the hymns for musical performance, which are generically called shabad. These consist of a number of short rhyming stanzas. The theme is set by the refrain, whose significance is emphasized by its often being composed in a somewhat different metre from the body of the hymn, and by its being followed in the text by the mark rahau or 'pause'. In most of the Gurus' hymns in the Adi Granth, the refrain comes after the first stanza, while those by Guru Tegh Bahadur and Guru Gobind Singh have the refrain at the beginning, following the more usual practice of Hindi poetry. The last verse is marked by the poetic signature 'Nanak'. Apart from the refrain, the metre and rhyme scheme are normally constant within a hymn. Many such formal patterns are used, with the primary separate classification in the arrangement of the Adi Granth being between the general body of hymns, typically in short four-line stanzas (*chaupade*), and hymns in eight stanzas of longer lines (*ashtapadian*).

Hymns of these types, their several subcategories and specially named variants, are followed in the different raga sections by the longer hymns. The best-represented type is the *var* or 'ballad', a genre used for heroic narrative in Punjabi folk poetry and adapted by the Gurus for the more extended and systematic expression of their teachings, especially the description and praise of manifestations of the divine creator. The titles of the original folk ballads to which each *var* is to be sung are recorded in the scriptural text. The basic structure of the *var* consists of some twenty or more stanzas called *pauri* or 'step', each written with some individual variation in the same metre and rhyme-scheme and containing the signature 'Nanak' in the final line. This second category of longer hymns designed to be sung also includes other examples of various individual types, each usually being made up of the rhymed stanzas characteristic of the *var*, and sometimes being united by the refrain which is a characteristic feature of the *shabad*.

The third formal category is typically the shortest. All the teachers of medieval north India used brief one-off verses for the direct and pithy expression of their teachings, their insights, their critiques of the human condition, and their commentaries on verses by other masters. Kabir's reputation in particular rests on his mastery of this genre, which in the Adi Granth is called *shalok*. At its shortest, a *shalok* normally consists of a pair of rhyming lines, each divided by quite a strong internal caesura, making four syntactic units in all. Some *shaloks* are considerably longer this, but whatever the length the last line typically begins with the poetic signature. Unlike the genres so far considered, the *shalok* is essentially something to be remembered and repeated orally, rather than recited in sung performance. In Guru Arjan's edition of the Adi Granth, however, most of the *shaloks* by the earlier Gurus were inserted into the *vars*, just as in folk poetry the sung stanzas of the heroic ballad were linked by narrative recitative. The authorship of each *shalok* is separately indicated in the text by the appropriate numerical formula M1, M2, etc., but they are typically placed without regard to the chronological sequence of their composition to offer some sort of commentary on the following *pauri*. Thus, while Guru Arjan composed original *shaloks* to go with his own *vars*, the *vars* by other Gurus are composite works in their canonical form. Those *shaloks* for which no home was found in the *vars* were placed in the concluding third section of the Adi Granth.

Finally, there is a variety of compositions which resemble the *shalok* in not being designed for musical performance, but which are like the *var* in their extended length. The Adi Granth, which otherwise contains few instances of this type, begins with the outstanding example of Guru Nanak's *Japji*, uniquely composed in stanzas of subtly varied rhythm as a litany for private recitation. The Dasam Granth contains many more examples, including the *Zafarnama*, which is composed in rhyming couplets, in the style of Persian epic poetry. More is said about the structure of these and the other longer compositions translated in this volume in the short introductions to them in the main text.

Having outlined the main features of the forms in which they are expressed, we may now turn to consider the chief emphases of the Gurus' teachings.

0.2.2 Content

Although not set out in the form of a systematic treatise, the teachings of Guru Nanak which are the central inspiration of the Sikh scriptures are encapsulated in extended compositions such as the *Japji*, which appears as the first item selected for translation in this volume.

The *Japji* is recited daily by Sikhs, and its opening formula, the *Mul Mantar* or 'foundational statement', serves as the Sikh credo insofar as it articulates the nature of the divine as experienced by Nanak:

ik oankar, satnam, karta purakh, nirbhau, nirvair, akal murat, ajuni, saibhang, gurprasad.

This statement is often translated in conformity to the rationalized idiom of monotheism as follows:

One God/Reality Exists, Whose Name is True, Creative Power,

Without Fear, Without Enmity, Timeless Form, Unborn, Self-Existent, By the Guru's Grace.

Of special importance is the opening phrase ik oankar (better trans-lated as: 'One, Manifest as Word') which consists of the numeral 1, universally recognizable across cultures and languages, followed by the sign oan (lit. the unfolding as Word) and completed by the extended sign -kar which connects oan to the next two words in the Mul Mantar: sat (from the Sanskrit satya 'existence, being') followed by nam (literally 'Name').

The verse following the Mul Mantar further elaborates the nature of the Absolute One as:

> True in the beginning, True before time began,
> He is True, Nanak, and ever will be True.

However, an important question arises here. If, as Nanak claims, the truth of this Absolute One can be experienced here and now, what is it that stops each and every person from realizing this all the time? The answer for Guru Nanak is relatively straightforward. From the standpoint of someone who has actualized the divine in his or her own existence, the Absolute is One (ik), but the stand-point from which humans normally relate to this One prevents them from actualizing this Oneness within their existence. According to Guru Nanak this standpoint that we regard as normality is in fact mediated through the ego or the self which asserts its own individuality (haumai or 'self-attachment', the sense of 'I am my own self' or 'I am self-existent'), that is, its oneness and propriety as the prior basis for all relationality per se. By reproducing this self as an identity that sets itself in opposition to anything that is differ-ent, the ego maintains its existence by erecting barriers against the outside world. It sees itself as a subject fundamentally separated from everything else which becomes an object for it. This subject/object mode of relating is what Guru Nanak terms as duality (dubidha).

But the problem, as Nanak sees it, goes much further than the simple assumption that the ego is the source of all duality. For as he explains in the first stanza of Japji (see 1.1 in the translation below), from the standpoint of the ego, the Absolute cannot be attained either through conceptual thought or through ritual purity no matter how much one thinks or engages in ritual. Nor can the Absolute be obtained by practising silent austerities since these too fail to silence the ego's incessant chatter, nor indeed by satisfying one's innermost cravings. The ego works by routing our experience of the Absolute through concepts, rituals and austerities. As a result the Absolute is never experienced as such, only re-presented as an object or idol to constantly gratify the ego's desire for permanence or absolute self-identity. How then does one overcome egotism and achieve self-realization? How can the ego's illusory barriers be broken?

Guru Nanak answers this at the end of the first and second stanzas (1.1–2). The ego's wall is broken by orienting the self towards a divine imperative that is always already inscribed with the self. But in order to understand and follow this imperative, the ego itself must become silent so that one no longer says 'I am my self'. For Guru Nanak, this silencing of the ego is not to be understood literally. Silence refers to a process of withdrawal at the very moment that the self *names* itself as 'I' – where 'I' is understood as the origin or starting-point in any relationship to an other. To assert one's existence in this world through *self*-naming is, for Nanak, a fundamental misuse of language the essence of which is the 'Name (*nam*) and the work of naming as such.

So the problem and its solution, according to Guru Nanak, lies in understanding the nature of the ego. From the standpoint of the ego reality is perceived dualistically in terms of either/or distinctions such as One/Many, life/death, existence/non-existence, form/formlessness, good/evil, time/eternity, transcendence/immanence, etc. Perhaps the most telling of all such binary oppositions is the characterization of the Absolute as having form or qualities as opposed to being formless or without qualities, a distinction that arises from the standpoint of ontological separation between man and divine. Such a standpoint, however, replaces the immediate experience of the One with the dualistic re-presentation of that experience. For Nanak the experience of the One cannot be attained by simply overcoming such binaries either through annihilation of opposites, or by elevating one term over the other. Rather the unity proper to the Absolute can only be represented as paradox, namely, the intersection, coincidence and interplay of opposites.

The divine is infinitely distant (absent) but immediately accessible (present). Yet distance and accessibility, absence and presence
become meaningful only in relation to an ego that has become a
stranger to itself – once again a paradox. If the paradox is accepted,
though, knowledge of the Absolute as One comes to be seen as
inseparable from the experience of freedom (mukti) exemplified
through all manner of co-dependent relationships based on the
communion of love between divine and human, but which extends
equally to the love between individual human beings and to the
love between humans and the world in general. As an example of
this the Sikh Gurus often invoke the classic imagery of separation
and fusion between the lover and the beloved: the virgin bride who
anticipates the embrace of the bridegroom on her wedding night,
or the wife's longing for her husband's return from a far-off land.
Bride, wife and virgin are metaphors for the self which is individuated and which pines for union with the other which is divine. The
re-joining of the two is the Absolute as One. To achieve union the
self must relinquish its individuality so that the mind (man, literally
'heart' or 'soul') can emerge as the lover able to merge with the
beloved. This state of fusion where knowledge becomes non-
knowledge is not a metaphysical ideal but a lived reality in which
the liberated person instinctively avoids relating to everything else
in terms of subject–object duality. Such a realized being no longer
re-presents the Absolute since the conscious distinction between
self and other, I and not-I, lover and beloved has disappeared leaving an ecstatic and purely spontaneous form of existence (sahaj).

In Sikh tradition, a person thus liberated from the bonds of
individuatedness is known as a gurmukh (lit. one whose existence is
centred around the guru) in contradistinction from the manmukh
(lit. one whose existence is self-centred). The distinction between
gurmukh and manmukh is not simply an ethical one, since 'ethics'
implies some minimal binding to a structure of the self in the form
of law or duty. Rather the distinction implies a freedom from the
bindings of the self which in turn gives rise not to an annihilation
of the self as might be thought from the perspective of rational
logic, but to a spontaneity of action–speech–thought. Whereas the
manmukh's action, speech and thought remain tied to self-
consciousness, the gurmukh constantly struggles for release from the
mechanism of self-attachment (haumai) giving rise to an intensely

creative mode of existence that is aligned with the divine imperative (hukam).

In Guru Nanak's philosophy, whether it is seen epistemologically as a shift from duality to Oneness, or existentially as one from gurmukh to manmukh, the transition itself revolves around the efficacy of the Name (nam), which is both the object of love and the means of loving attachment to the beloved. As Guru Nanak says in Japji (1.32):

> If this one tongue became a hundred thousand,
> If they in turn were multiplied by twenty,
> They would take a hundred thousand times
> To praise the one Name of the Lord.
> This is the way to climb the stairs
> That lead to union with Him.

As the point of contact between the human and the divine, between transcendence and immanence, the One and the All, the Name is simultaneously the privileged medium for experiencing the condition of non-duality, and the mechanism by which the ego can be liberated from its tendency for self-attachment. Attunement to Name constitutes a wordless communication, or rather a partaking of love between self and mind or soul, which corresponds to the primordial love through which all existent things relate to each other before individuation takes over (1.4).

In Guru Nanak's hymns the Name (nam) is not a particular word or mantra. It is inscribed within, yet comprises the vibration of the cosmos. As the constituting link between mystic interiority and worldly action, the Name is appropriated by the gurmukh through the practice of constantly holding in mind the Name (nam simaran) – a form of meditation in which the One simultaneously becomes the focus of an individual's awareness and his motivation to perform righteous deeds. But the Name cannot be obtained voluntarily. Its attainment depends on the grace or favourable glance (kirpa, nadar) of a spiritual preceptor or guru. Nanak's own preceptor, however, was not a personal guru but an impersonal principle: the divine that manifests outwardly in ordinary human language as Word (shabad), but which manifests inwardly as satguru or the divine principle to which the individual mind can form a personal relationship. It needs to be noted, however, that distinctions such as inner/outer, personal/impersonal are moot from the standpoint of one who has realized Oneness.

A variation on the terms *shabad* and *satguru* which denote an internalized Word, is the term *anhad shabad* or *anhad nad* (literally, 'the unspoken Word' or 'the unstruck Sound') inherited by the Sikh Gurus from their predecessors, the Sants such as Kabir, who in turn borrows the term from the Siddhas and the Naths, the expert practitioners of Hatha Yoga. According to the Nath usage the term *anhad shabad* refers to the mystical sound that is heard at the climax of the Hatha Yoga process. In the context of the Sants and the Sikh Gurus, the term refers to words or language that are not tainted by traces of ego and therefore not subject to ordinary communication in which words are merely labels for things. Once a word is identified with a thing, that thing can be turned into objective information which can be transferred or communicated between one ego and another.

As *anhad shabad* the Word itself speaks or resounds without being spoken, which sounds like a tautology but in fact indicates a mode of communication where the ego no longer controls the production of words, nor indeed the process of making words into things. Removed from the grasp of the ego, words are no longer given value according to their degree of correspondence to things, but instead arise from an internalized mode of speech that occurs between mind-as-ego and mind-as-soul. The unspoken Word arises from a mode of communication in which the mind speaks with itself, giving the impression of a departure from the standards of everyday social reality in which speech is meaningful if it makes sense to everybody. The point of this seemingly impossible communication is in effect to rejoin the two aspects of the dualistic mind separated by ego sense. Devoid of ego traces, the Word that is so minted in the mind appears as an expression of wonder (*vismad*) that is attuned to all of nature's wonderful workings. Just as all creation is simply happening without asking why, so the unspoken Word arises without connection to intention, desire or will (1.4).

Thus, for Guru Nanak, the divine as guru (*satguru*) manifests as Word (*shabad*) that can be heard, accepted by the mind and turned into loving devotion (1.21):

> Hearing, acceptance, love in the heart
> Show the place for true bathing and cleansing within.

Or again (1.38):

> In love as the vessel, the Name is dissolved,
> Producing the Word in the mint that is true.

Connecting to what was said earlier, the reorientation in consciousness that the Sikh Gurus are looking for must happen primarily at the level of language or Word (*shabad*), such that one's ordinary relationship to language, which is based on *self*-naming where the 'I' is attached to itself via a primary identification with its own name, is transformed through attunement to the Word of the Guru (*shabad-guru*) which revolves around the Name through which all creation expresses its link to the divine source. The Sikh Gurus speak of this principle in different ways and in different contexts. Consequently the terms *nam*, *shabad* and *guru* are regarded as virtually synonymous as well as the mystical source of authority in Sikhism.

Name, as the Sikh Gurus articulate it, perfectly illustrates the paradox of the One and the Many. It cannot, for example, simply be reduced to *God's* Name or to the names of individual gods. Throughout the scriptures the term *nam* serves to replace what is named in other religious and philosophical traditions as the entity 'God' whose name is no more than a tool for calling this entity to mind at will. In contradistinction, *nam* makes superfluous the need for such an entity which is in effect no more than a macroscopic manifestation of the ego. Thus, whereas human ego is the microcosm, the entity 'God' is simply the macrocosmic Ego. For the Gurus this is to remain subject to the operation of *maya*, the veil of ignorance generated by the ego. Notwithstanding the fact that 'God' is referred to as the highest, the ultimate, etc., these superlatives still only refer to a highest or ultimate entity, which would remain within a scale determined by man, albeit a scale that spans from the lowest to the highest. 'God', in other words, is made into a thing like any other thing, subject to conception in terms of subject/object duality and, therefore, never experienced as such.

Yet experience is the only way of relating to the Name. This is conditioned by the intricate relationship between ego and Name, to which the Gurus devoted many verses. In contradistinction to the 'I' generated by ego's craving, which is regarded by the Gurus in their explorations of the opposition between Name and ego as operating an economy of narcissism precisely in order to gain a return to one-self, Name is the only capital that cannot be reduced to the status of a thing and circulated in an economy of exchange. The Gurus' instruction in this regard is very pragmatic: one cannot simply escape the economic nature of one's existence in the world driven by the self's desire to make everything its own property. But it is possible to change the very nature of this economy by transforming narcissistic self-love into a love for the Name.

Moreover, the Gurus suggest a practice for transforming the ego-based economy of ordinary life in which we accumulate knowledge and exchange of entities, enact commercial transactions, reasonable rules, plans and projects, religious rites and rituals. This practice is *nam simaran*: the constant holding in remembrance of the Name, which goes beyond ritualistic repetition to become a spontaneous form of loving meditation in which the ego is disappropriated. The paradoxical dialectic here between the appropriation of Name and the disappropriation of ego becomes more evident from the etymology of the word *simaran*. Derived from the Indo-European root *smr-* 'remember, hold in mind', the term has traditionally been understood to resonate with the Sanskrit terms *mr-* and *marana*, to die or to pass away, suggesting that *simaran* is a form of remembrance which automatically lets go or renounces. Stated differently, *simaran* is first of all remembrance of one's own mortality, of the ego's death, remembering which one awakens to the Name and attains peace. As Guru Arjan writes in his great composition *Sukhmani Sahib* (Adi Granth, p. 292):

> Remember, remember the One whose remembrance
>   brings peace,
> By dispelling the body's pain and anxiety of death.

This deeper meaning of *nam simaran* was enacted by Guru Gobind Singh in his creation of the Khalsa. For the person who craves to drink the nectar of the Name (*amrit*) must first surrender the ego if he or she is to receive not only the *amrit* whose essence is the Name, but a new self under the name Singh for men or Kaur for women, imparted through the initiation of the double-edged sword (khande di pahul). Far from being a dramatic departure, Guru Gobind Singh's administering of amrit to the Khalsa can be interpreted as a re-enactment of Guru Nanak's initial initiation into the Name at Sultanpur.

Because nam simaran is not a metaphysical concept but a concrete sacrificial practice for transforming memory, as that function of mind which weaves time into the structures that manipulate our existence and thinking, it can also be viewed as a way of transforming worldly time and existence. It provides a means for the individual to actively participate in the world and to change whatever destiny had been inscribed onto the self as it passed through different existences and life forms accumulating karmic traces. The experience of the Name attained through the constant practice of simaran erases the production of karmic traces thereby transforming the mechanical existence of the manmukh into the spontaneous activity of a gurmukh. Thus, from the standpoint of the gurmukh, such conceptual dualities as those between religion and politics or between mysticism and violence become superfluous. This is evident in the lives of the Sikh Gurus for whom there was no contradiction between mystical experience and the life of a soldier or a householder.

0.2.3 Commentary and Translation

In itself, the closure of the text implied by formation of the scriptural canon can be seen as a limitation, but it is counterbalanced by the process of exposition and interpretation which began at an early stage in the evolution of the Sikh tradition. This process has continued throughout the succeeding centuries, and has been marked since the later nineteenth century by the publication in printed form of a very substantial body of commentary and of numerous translations, especially into English.

Given that this process of reflecting on the bani or Word begins with the Sikh Gurus themselves who sought to clarify the meanings of certain words and themes contained in the hymns of their predecessors, it can also be seen as a way of naturally extending or rendering porous the borders of the canon. However, the first systematic interpretation of the Gurus' teachings effectively begins with the writings of two of Guru Arjan's contemporaries, one his rival and the other his chief disciple. Miharban, the son of Prithi Chand, Guru Arjan's older brother and rival claimant to the Guruship, wrote probably the first extended commentary on Guru Nanak's Japji, choosing prose as his medium. Due to his father's schismatic position, however, this work has been largely disregarded within mainstream Sikh tradition. Bhai Gurdas was Guru Arjan's chosen amanuensis and insofar as his own writings faithfully conveyed the letter and spirit of the Guru's teaching, they have long been considered to hold the key to understanding the Adi Granth as guide for living.

Despite the fact that the works of these two seventeenth-century figures indicate the existence at the time of a tradition of scriptural commentary, there was no further systematic or sustained attempt at the exposition of the teachings of the Sikh Gurus for over a century. In fact we have to wait till the late eighteenth and early nineteenth centuries for the next sustained exposition of Sikh scripture, which occurs in the works of scholars belonging to the Nirmala, Udasi and Giani schools of interpretation. These were all strongly affected by Brahminical and, particularly, Vedantic modes of interpretation and were especially influential during the final decades of the pre-colonial period. The Nirmala and Udasi schools rose to prominence in Sikh religious affairs primarily as the result of Maharaja Ranjit Singh's reign in the early nineteenth century. Many leading representatives of the Udasi and Nirmala school were patronized by the Sikh nobility or employed as attendants and readers of the Adi Granth at various Sikh religious establishments. It was the Nirmala schools in particular that revived interest in the work of analysing scriptural meanings, albeit from within a Vedantic perspective.

However, the true renaissance of scriptural exegesis, and ironically the effective closure of the Nirmala and Udasi influence, is associated with the scholars of the Singh Sabha, a social and religious reformist movement which emerged during the late nineteenth and early twentieth centuries to achieve a dominant position during the colonial era. Indeed the development of Sikhism, after the death of Maharaja Ranjit Singh and the fall of the Lahore Darbar, can be linked to the new status of the Sikhs as one of many colonized groups in India. As a relatively small minority even within the

Punjab to which they were largely confined, the Sikhs were faced not only with the direct challenge of a European colonial state and the entry into modernity, but also with the secondary challenge of an active and resurgent neo-Hinduism. It fell to the lay leadership of the Lahore Singh Sabha, as opposed to the more aristocratic Amritsar Singh Sabha, to articulate the main Sikh response to the general challenges of modernity while at the same time mounting a defence against hostile takeover by a politicized Hinduism. The response of the Lahore Singh Sabha intellectuals (with whom the title 'Singh Sabha' became virtually synonymous) was to reformulate an interpretation of Sikhism based on the ideal of the Tat Khalsa, the 'real Khalsa' as defined by the reformists to conform with the categories of interpretation encouraged by the colonial state. This distinguished Sikhism from Hinduism as an ethical monotheism closely linked to a separate scripture. It was the Adi Granth as Guru Granth Sahib whose unique authority thus unequivocally guaranteed Sikhism's separate status as a fully scriptural religion, or a real 'religion of the Book'.

Besides its central programme of enforcing unambiguous notions of religious authority and community, a renewed understanding of Sikh scripture became an important part of their overall project to emphasize the distinctiveness of Sikhism as a separate religious tradition. Recognizing the problems caused by the archaism of its language, the Singh Sabha intellectuals encouraged a congruence of religious and ethnic identity by, for the first time, developing Punjabi in the sacred Gurmukhi script as a vehicle for modern literature. This development was in clear distinction from the Punjabi Muslims' espousal of Urdu as the chief cultural language of Islam in India and the neo-Hindu Arya Samaj's strong support for Hindi. The reformists therefore put great efforts into the production of commentaries and other reference materials in modern Punjabi. Guided by the rationalistic spirit of Western education, a natural consequence of this reform movement was, on the one hand, a total displacement of the Nirmala and Udasi literature, and on the other, a transformation of the older Giani style of exegesis by infusing it with modern rationalistic tools of analysis. One of the main outcomes of the Singh Sabha movement was a series of detailed scriptural commentaries through which the reformists aimed to recapture the original spirit of the Gurus' teachings as contained in the Adi Granth.

The Singh Sabha's ideal of recapturing the original teachings of the Sikh Gurus was, however, dependent on showing that these commentaries were not in any way a transformation of tradition, but rather a re-forming or returning of the tradition back to an original intention. While the reformers thus thought of themselves as faithfully mirroring Guru Nanak's central teachings, closer scrutiny shows that the writing of the scriptural commentaries was conceived as a long-term project, motivated primarily as a reaction to the new era in which the representation of Sikh teachings through English had assumed a crucial importance.

For the Sikhs this new era proved a rude awakening. Since Sikhism had long remained intrinsically linked to its homeland in the Punjab, there was never any strong incentive in earlier centuries to disturb the close association of scripture with liturgy by encouraging translations of the Adi Granth. But now for the first time Sikhs were forced to come face to face with the dangers as well as the possibilities of translation, where the stakes were nothing less than a displacement of the indigenous categories for representing the Adi Granth in favour of the conceptual categories of the West. The publication in 1877 of the first major English translation of substantial sections of the Adi Granth by the German missionary Ernest Trumpp can be considered an 'event' of cultural translation that continues to cast a shadow on all modern translations and representations of Sikh scripture. For this reason alone, Trumpp's version merits some attention.

Trumpp's basic thesis was that although the 'chief point in Nanak's doctrine' was the 'unity of the Supreme Being', there were no reasonable grounds for specifically differentiating the notion of 'Supreme Being' in the Adi Granth from orthodox Hindu philosophy. Clearly influenced by the Brahminical leanings of his Nirmala collaborators, Trumpp translated the first line of the Adi Granth by missing out the numeral 1, rendering the syllable ik oankar as om. Since philosophers of Vedanta had long expounded the meaning of om in terms of the Hindu trinity of Brahma, Vishnu, Shiva, for Indologists om symbolized Hindu pantheism, whereas for missionaries it represented the inability of the Hindu mind to transcend multiplicity and achieve a sufficiently monotheistic concept of the divine. Once a lack of theological transcendence was established in this manner, it was but a short step to designate the rest of Sikh scripture as lacking any systematic conceptual unity.

For reformist Sikhs in the late nineteenth century, such a portrayal of the Adi Granth threatened to undermine the image of Sikhism in the minds of the very colonial administrators who had commissioned Trumpp's translation in order to better understand the Sikh religion's fundamental doctrines. By asserting that Nanak's teaching was rooted philosophically in Vedantic monism and religiously in Hindu pantheism, it suggested that earlier European accounts of Sikhism as a 'moralizing Deism' were largely mistaken. More importantly, perhaps, Trumpp's work transferred the conceptual terminology for representing the Adi Granth on to a comparative grid that was, on the one hand, historicist in that it classified religions on a scale of conceptual evolution, and on the other hand philosophico-theological, insofar as the degree of its evolution was measured in terms of divine transcendence, the standard for which was of course the God of Christian philosophy.

Future Sikh translators and interpreters were thus presented with a clearly defined task. This was to prove that their sacred scripture could yield both a concept of God that was suitably transcendent and a system of ethics in keeping with this. Trumpp's conceptual demarcation had provided a framework which future translators could contest but which they could neither ignore nor remain unaffected by. In order to refute him it would be necessary first to immerse oneself in and adopt the premises of Western philosophical theology.

Perhaps the best examples of this attempt are the translations from the scriptures by Macauliffe, included in his six-volume study of The Sikh Religion published in 1909. Unlike his predecessor, Macauliffe opted to disperse translations of key hymns from the Adi Granth and Dasam Granth within traditional narratives and legends of the lives of the Sikh Gurus. The general accuracy of Macauliffe's translation was eulogized by leading Sikh reformists and traditional scholars, and even today his work remains useful as an anthology of scriptural hymns. It is however far from clear whether his attempt to rescue Sikhism from Trumpp's main charge that Sikhism was mere pantheism actually succeeded. Indeed Macauliffe quite plainly admits failure in dissociating Sikh theism from pantheism, when he remarks in his introduction: 'No religious teacher has succeeded in logically dissociating theism from pantheism. In some passages of the Gurus' writings pantheism is, as we have seen, clearly implied, while in other texts is made distinct from the creator . . .' (Macauliffe, Sikh Religion, vol. 1, p. lxiii).

Even though Macauliffe faithfully mirrored the views of the reformist Sikh collaborators with whom he worked so closely, the conceptual terminology of his critique of Trumpp was intimately conditioned by the very schema used by his predecessor. The reason for this is fairly obvious. The moment that Sikh scripture is translated into a European language, it must coexist in a terrain where all talk of religion or of God is automatically routed through the categories of Christian philosophical theology. Thus, the only difference between the two was the position and status that each attributed to Sikhism in the evolution of religions, which for Macauliffe was full-fledged theism, for Trumpp a pantheism. Macauliffe's translation helped the reformists to satisfy their desire, denied by Trumpp, to prove a 'sufficiently exalted idea of God' in the Sikh scriptures.

The ultimate fulfilment of this desire could, however, only be attained by proving that such an idea of God already existed within their own scripture and in its native language. This was the task that fell not only to the writers of the exegetical commentaries on the Adi Granth which emerged more than fifty years after Trumpp's translation, but also to Sikhs undertaking the translation of the Adi Granth into English. Many such commentaries in modern Punjabi and translations into English, including ambitious undertakings covering the entire scripture as well as numerous works devoted to selected compositions, have been produced since the early twentieth century. In this process the primary role has been played by the commentaries which have aimed to provide an 'authentic' meaning for scripture, as it were a direct link to the particularity of the Gurus' intentions. The translations, which have largely been the work of Indian scholars educated in English but intellectually inspired by these commentaries, can be seen as a way of projecting these aims to an increasingly global Anglophone audience, thereby providing evidence for the Sikh claim to the universality of their Gurus' teachings, and their distinctiveness from Hinduism.

Traditional Sikh historiography has portrayed the Singh Sabha scholars as having saved Sikhism from the clutches of an increasingly assertive Hinduism. But it has to be recognized that the very means which they used to combat Hinduism, through the projection of a Sikh theology based on a dichotomy between God and man or world, and underpinned by a conception of God's identity as totally transcendent, are themselves drawn from the tradition of Christian theology.

A closer look at the scriptural text suggests that in many respects Guru Nanak's teachings represented precisely the opposite of this dichotomy. Unlike the modern reformist commentators, Guru Nanak does not show himself to have been concerned with establishing theological proofs of God's identity. Rather than emphasizing a 'God's eye view' from the standpoint of eternity, the Adi Granth in fact repeatedly stresses that it is precisely duality which prevents man from achieving the fundamental purpose of life, namely, union with the divine. Duality of the kind intrinsic to the reformist theology adopted from Christian intellectual traditions is repeatedly castigated by the Gurus as a projection of the ego, in which the ego deludes itself into thinking it is at the centre of all experience.

This generates the illusion of individuality and eternally fixed identity that is, ironically, exemplified by modern Sikhism's self-representation as a nation, and the politics of Sikh nationalism in the twentieth century. Though rarely acknowledged, Sikh nationalism in the late twentieth century has drawn silently but profusely on the Singh Sabha's reconfiguration of the Adi Granth's religious ideas. However, the rise and fall of Sikh nationalism in the previous century illustrates the rule that formerly successful solutions may not always prove readily adaptable to changed circumstances and contexts. Definitions of authority and community were well devised by the Singh Sabha movement to maintain the independent development of a religion and its institutions in a colonial environment and to help lead these into the different circumstances of post-coloniality. But they have proved much less adequate for generating responses to the very different contexts of diasporic Sikhs living in Western societies or of a new generation of Sikhs growing up in a rapidly urbanizing and modernizing India.

Given that Sikhs and Sikhism will continue to look to their scripture as a source of responses to their post-colonial predicament, perhaps the time has arrived to question the way in which the reception and self-representation of Sikh scripture into the West continues to organize itself around the politics of nationalism. It could be argued that the central themes of Sikh scripture actually resist both the intellectual demands of Western categorization, which are based on the priority given to conscious reflexivity, and the cultural demands of the nation as its central organizing concept. Once such questions are raised, it may be seen that even the most recent translations of Sikh scripture have continued to be unable to refuse the seductions of the neo-colonial schema. While we would not claim that the present volume has been entirely unable to escape from the constraints imposed by the history of translating Sikh scripture, the selection and arrangement of its contents, as well as its overall rationale and translation strategies, have nevertheless been conceived in a conscious awareness of the pitfalls that may thereby be so readily stumbled into.

0.3 Approaching the Gurus' Teachings

0.3.1 Arrangement

The approach to the Gurus' teachings which is presented in this volume itself of course reflects the early twenty-first-century situation of its compilers, who are each professionally employed in Western universities on either side of the Atlantic and who have brought to their collaboration the dynamic tensions which naturally arise from the not always wholly convergent perspectives of different generations and different intellectual preoccupations.

In developing our approach we have sought at all stages to learn from the varied solutions arrived at by earlier translators. Since we never intended a complete translation of the vast corpus of the Sikh scriptures, issues of selection and presentation demanded much attention from the outset, even before beginning the actual work of translation itself. The different approaches to selection adopted by our predecessors have included attempts to provide a proportional selection from all the Gurus, sometimes also from the compositions of the Bhagats, as well as decisions to concentrate upon those items which are particularly familiar from their liturgical use, and various combinations of these. Similarly, the presentation in a printed format readily accessible to English readers of a selection of hymns detached from the original context of their masterfully organized musical arrangement has presented all translators with another set of issues to decide. Previous approaches have sometimes sought to provide the necessary new context by linking the hymns to traditional non-scriptural narrative, as Macauliffe did, or by taking an historical approach, or else simply through a general introduction supplemented by notes.

As the title of this volume indicates, our own selection has been governed by a primary focus upon the instructional rather than the lyrical aspect of the Gurus' compositions. In terms of genres, this emphasis has naturally led us to select particularly from the short *shaloks* in which the Gurus' teachings are typically expressed with pointedly direct force. While we have also set out to include reasonably representative complete samples of other genres, rather than looking to take individual verses out of the context of their original setting, here too the emphasis has been on examples with a strong and clear teaching message.

In terms of the proportional representation of individual Gurus, we have like all our predecessors at every stage been drawn to the special power and originality of Guru Nanak's compositions, so these find a particularly prominent place in our selection too. We have however also tried to give suitable, if not always strictly proportional, emphasis to the compositions of the later Gurus whose works are included in the Adi Granth, and we have included two significant items by Guru Gobind Singh to give some idea of Sikhism's other scripture, the Dasam Granth.

All translators of this material have recognized that the modern English reader needs some help in understanding it. In order to avoid the misleading device of silently inserting surreptitious commentary into the translations themselves in a well-meant effort to make their meaning more transparent to the contemporary reader, we have sought to supplement translations which are as direct as possible with a good deal of introductory material, both here and at intervals throughout the main text of the volume.

Our translations are grouped into eleven sections, whose rationale is explained below. Each section is provided with its own short introduction. For ease of reference, numbers have been provided for all shorter items as they appear within the sections, while the verses of longer compositions are numbered as in the original.

Following standard practice, all textual references to the Adi Granth include both an abbreviated description and the page number on which the item begins, so e.g. 'Srirag M1 24, p. 23' indicates the 24th *shabad* by Guru Nanak in Srirag, printed on p. 23. The abbreviations A and C are used to indicate *ashtapadi* and *chhant* respectively. Further abbreviations are used to indicate *shaloks* included in the *vars* of the Adi Granth, so e.g. 'Sarang ki Var, M3 33.1, p. 1250' indicates the *shalok* by Guru Amar Das included as the first *shalok* before the 33rd stanza of the *var* in Sarang (itself composed by Guru Ram Das), printed on p. 1250. Since the sectional introductions are intended to provide the necessary context, the endnotes which accompany the translations have been kept to a minimum, with proper names being listed in the glossary at the end of the volume.

0.3.2 Rationale

The underlying rationale of our translation is expressed in its arrangement into sections. These are of two types, with the six odd-numbered sections (1, 3, 5, 7, 9, 11) consisting of single major compositions by the Gurus arranged in broadly chronological order, while the five even-numbered sections (2, 4, 6, 8, 10) contain selections of shorter compositions which are each arranged around a major theme. The ongoing dynamic between the two types is deliberately intended to bring out the inherent tensions between form and theme, as indeed between history and timelessness, which have shaped the tradition.

Not much needs to be said here about the individual items contained in the six odd-numbered sections, since each begins with its own introduction. Overall, the six major compositions selected are intended to provide some overview of the evolution of the Gurus' teachings through time. The first three items are all by Guru Nanak, beginning with his *Japji* (1), about whose primal significance in the Sikh tradition as well in daily Sikh ritual practice something has already been said. The next odd-numbered text is his hardly less important *Asa ki Var* (3), here presented in its original format of stanzas only, without the *shaloks* by Guru Nanak and Guru Angad which were subsequently added to create its present familiar form, although a number of these are included in the thematic sections.

The final long item linked to Guru Nanak is the *Siddh Gosht* (5), cast in the unusual format of a dialogue with the yogic masters called Siddhs in which the Guru's teachings are set out with particular relation to conventional understandings of yoga.

The other three longer items are by later Gurus. The *Anand Sahib* (7), which is the best-known composition by Guru Amar Das, provides a peculiarly interesting illustration of the way in which the Gurus' teachings, while continuing the original message of Guru Nanak, also come to address the different circumstances created by the leadership of a growing and organized community of followers. After considerable discussion, we took the difficult decision not to include one of the many longer compositions by Guru Arjan, partly on the grounds of the very length of such extended hymns as the *Sukhmani Sahib*, deciding instead to acknowledge his importance through appropriate selection from his shorter compositions in the thematic sections, each of which ends with a piece by him.

The two final odd-numbered items are each by Guru Gobind Singh and are taken from the Dasam Granth. Together they show how the Gurus' emphasis had shifted over the seventeenth century and had come to confront in their own languages some of the values of the religiously determined high cultures of the time. The set of hymns entitled *Shabad Hazare* (*Patshahi* 10), included as item 9, uses Braj Bhasha to question Hindu practices and belief, while Persian is the medium adopted for the *Zafarnama* (11). Cast as a letter in verse by Guru Gobind Singh addressed to the emperor Aurangzeb, this final item brings the timelessness of the Gurus' teachings firmly into the world of historical time.

Somewhat more needs to be said about the five thematic sections, whose definition and arrangement has been consciously devised to address the issues raised in the discussion above of the continuing implications of the Singh Sabha reformists' fundamental rewriting of the Gurus' teachings.

Several interlinked considerations have guided the selection and organization of the themes identified in this volume. The first consideration was how to respect the traditional status of the scripture, on the one hand, as a canonical text (the Granth as Guru), and on the other hand, as the inspired Word (*shabad-guru*). The key to maintaining this dual aspect is to recognize that the Adi Granth, at least, poses a certain resistance to being split into aesthetic and intellectual components respectively, which has led to an increasing separation between the musical component, regarded as sensuous owing to its performative, decorative and figural aspects, and the intellectual component of theology, grammar, etc., which gives rise to meanings. This resistance is still very much evident today when one considers that the primary contact with the main body of the text (i.e. the non-liturgical sections) occurs through a combination of performance (*kirtan*) and exposition (*viakhia*), both live and supplemented through technology as on audio-visual tapes, DVD, radio, TV and internet. What marks out this sort of text reception is a production of meaning that is inspired and provoked by the aesthetic component which helps to loosen the teleological and rational leanings of the nationalized idiom. Because the pure element of the aesthetic is time, a certain resistance will be posed to any production of the figure of eternity, which enables the mind to focus more acutely on the nature of the present moment.

The focus on time brings us to our second consideration, which was to keep in mind the existential situation of the individual reader or listener. Though there is a strong emphasis in Sikh practice on communal singing and reciting of hymns, nevertheless, the text can only ever be appropriated and understood at the level of the individual. No two readers or listeners will ever imbibe exactly the same meaning, simply because the existential situation of one person is different from the next. Each individual comes into existence alone and must die alone. Though this point is rarely given the kind of attention it deserves, Sikh scripture repeatedly stresses the shortness of life and the ever-presence of death in life. The image of impermanence, transitoriness, the inevitability of returning to one's origin rather than an emphasis on eternity, should be considered the medium through which the Sikh Gurus have sought to remind the reader of the ego's fickleness. Reality as impermanence, the confrontation of the ego with time's loss, is therefore more than just a theme. It constitutes a structure-without-structure around which revolve the other themes described below. Equally important, it complements the aesthetics of the Adi Granth, since music's essential form is the playful movement of time.

The third consideration, which follows from the preceding two, was for our selection to highlight the sense of otherness in the teachings of the Sikh gurus. This emphasis on difference corresponds to a shift in the preoccupation of post-theistic religious studies away from historicism as the underlying universal of comparative religion towards a comparative enterprise that is more attentive to the voice of the particular. As argued above, the end result of the Sikh scriptures' movement into the Western frame was the projection of a 'positive' identity for the Adi Granth based on a desire to make its teachings fit into the emerging arena of 'world religions'. However, this 'identity', most noticeable as the schema of God versus World/Man outlined above, which is little more than a shadow of universalized Christian values, actually neutralizes the effect of the difference inherent in Sikh teachings. Thus the otherness of the Gurus' teachings resides in their ability to resist and infect the self-inoculating idiom of modernity and certain facile notions of pluralism and the 'dialogue' between cultures. The text's otherness can therefore be considered in terms of the ability of the teachings to live on, to survive in and through translation.

The above considerations are exemplified in our deliberate selection of themes which attempt to address the context of a post-colonial English-speaking diaspora. The themes that we have selected are: Impermanence: The Gift and Curse of Time (2); Mind, Self, Ego (4); Ethical Being: Action and Grace (6); Guru as Word: The Location of Authority (8); Communicating Ecstasy: Knowledge and Non-Knowledge (10).

Clearly these titles represent a shift from the tightly organized schema adopted by the Singh Sabha scholars which imbibed and mirrored the Western conceptualization of religion. One of the main concerns in making our thematic selections was to emphasize the interdependence and fluidity of these themes. They should not be considered as 'categories' of thought or judgement as understood within the Western philosophico-theological tradition. Categories are essentially ways of organizing reality according to certain divisions and thereby require some sort of transcendental apperception, the *a priori* unity of a transcendental self. For the Sikh Gurus, however, such a transcendental self can only exist on the field of the self-conscious mind. This field must be broken through in order to undergo actual experience of Oneness from which we have become increasingly separated as we go through life. Categories are no more than mental constructs subject to something more fundamental, namely, impermanence or the passage of time. The

Gurus' hymns by contrast are radically inter-categorical, emphasizing the fluid interplay and crossing of different themes within one underlying theme: the exhortation for man to experience liberation in and through the element of time and existence by recognizing the uncanny dialectic between the ego and the Name.

As our introductions to each set of selected hymns make clear, each theme is interlinked to the others. There is no hierarchy and no 'progression' from one to another. Each theme could easily provide an entry point to all of the others. The connection between them might easily be envisaged as a spiral that does not return to itself, as opposed to conceptual or categorical thought which returns full circle to its starting-point, the ego, thereby recuperating and accumulating the ego. Nevertheless our own arrangements suggest a possible movement from the experience of time as an existential awareness of one's own death (2), through a deepening reflection on the nature of mind, self and ego (4), towards a way of acting in deed, word and thought that is entirely spontaneous (6). The progressive renunciation of ego and movement towards spontaneity enables the mind to become a receptacle for the Word or Name as the location of authority which resides not in any time or place but in the figure of the gurmukh (8), who not only cultivates the highest state of mysticism but shows a profound will to communicate his or her ecstatic bliss with others (10). As explained in each of the summaries of leading ideas, all of these themes incorporate multiple other sub-themes that freely cross over from one main thematic section to another.

0.3.3 Translation Strategies

This concern to capture the original essence of the Gurus' teachings should, we strongly believe, be matched by an equal concern to try to reproduce at least some of the most salient features of the poetic form in which they are crucially expressed. Our translation strategies have been chiefly dictated by this aim. Like all translators, however, especially those working from texts originating at a quite considerable formal and cultural distance from modern English norms, we have also had to recognize that much was going to have to be sacrificed altogether and that much else was always going to be difficult to convey in a fully satisfactory way.

The main features of the original which have had to be lost at the outset in a translation into modern English are the whole musical dimension and the variations in languages which are both central to the medieval Indian context. It was also decided not to attempt any reproduction of the rhymes which are so prominent an organizing principle of all the original poetic forms, but which are so much harder to reproduce naturally in contemporary English. Not only is there an intrinsic paucity of available rhymes, as compared with the richness of the source languages, whether Punjabi, Hindi or Persian, but the systematic use of rhyme is all too liable to allow excessive pull to the target language by suggesting a similarity to the format of Christian hymns which would be quite inappropriate to our purpose.

We have, on the other hand, tried to do more systematic justice than some of our predecessors to other features of the original poetic structure. We have attached great importance to trying to convey the syntactic organization of the original as closely as possible. As has earlier been explained, the basic syntactic unit of the Guru's verse is confined to the compass of the line or half-line, and in order to keep their proportions as faithfully as we could, we have tried consistently to translate one such unit of expression in the original by one unit in English. While the temptation to expand on difficult half-lines is sometimes hard to resist, we have thought it more important to convey something of the difficulty intrinsically present in the extremely condensed expression sometimes favoured by the Gurus rather than to make everything misleadingly seem completely transparent on a first reading.

The gist of the overall content may be sensed to be quite clear, but in numerous places its detailed expression often gives rise to particular difficulties. These arise from the remarkable denseness and concision of expression which is made possible by the highly inflected language of the scriptures and which is such a conspicuous feature of Guru Nanak's style in particular, although instances are also found in the hymns of the later Gurus. Like all scriptural texts, quite a number of passages in the Adi Granth and Dasam Granth have continued to tax the most learned of commentators. In all such cases, where they seemed necessary to make the meaning clear in such instances, notes have been used to provide the necessary glosses.

We have also thought it important to underline the fact that the Gurus used poetry to communicate their teachings, by making our translations metrical. As in the originals, each composition is therefore normally translated into an internally consistent English metre, with deliberate changes of metrical pace being consciously reflected where they occur. Given the differences in poetic systems, it would be an unnatural exercise to try to reproduce the individual metres of the original. What we have aimed for, rather, is to convey the overall sense of formal pattern, sometimes for instance keeping the same number of metrical units as in the original but expanding the number of syllables by using anapaests (te-te-tum) rather than the standard iambic feet (te-tum). We have also availed ourselves of the metrical freedom to vary the length of the line by the addition of extra syllables where demanded by the sense, which was employed by all the earlier Gurus. The original schemes of metre and rhyme are explained in the introductions to the longer items.

In the case of the shorter compositions included in the thematic sections, while always keeping to our guiding principle of equivalence of syntactic units, divisions within lines are sometimes set out somewhat differently from those marked in the original. This has been done partly in order to give the reader pause by introducing some graphic variety on the printed page. As already explained, we have for the most part chosen to translate only complete compositions, and have normally indicated such formal features as the refrain in *shabads*, by the symbol R and indentation of the verse, or the placing of the poetic signature 'Nanak' in the final verse.

Modern English conventions make it necessary to add certain features which are not present in the original. The only punctuation in the Gurmukhi text of the scriptures is the double bar which marks the end of lines and verses. This is normally reproduced by a full stop in the translations, which however also use the usual range of punctuation marks to indicate other syntactic relationships. Like many non-roman scripts, Gurmukhi also lacks the distinction between upper and lower case letters, a feature which creates particular difficulties in a scriptural context with its own prior English conventions in this regard. We have been guided by the need for clarity, thus using capitals for epithets and pronouns relating to God, also for key terms in the Gurus' technical vocabulary like Name (*nam*) and Word (*shabad*), where we have aimed for a general consistency of rendering if not always strict one-to-one equivalence. Conversely, however, we have reserved the capitalized 'Guru' for the line of living Sikh Gurus, while the inner guide appears as 'guru' with lower case epithets and pronouns, thus allowing a distinction from those relating to God.

One other feature in which particular care has to be taken in producing a modern English translation of a pre-modern Indian original in such a way as to be properly sensitive to gender issues is that of the use of the third person pronouns. All the original languages have only a single form for the plural pronoun, like English 'they', and Persian has only a single form for the singular pronoun also. This gender-neutral convenience is however not available in English, with its threefold distinction of 'he, she, it', partly paralleled in pre-modern Punjabi and Hindi with their two-way distinction between masculine 'he (it)' and feminine 'she (it)'. The transcending of these categories which is our common modern ideal is thus intrinsically difficult. For reference to God, the use of the capitalized second person 'You' often achieves this, but there are many contexts which demand a third person pronoun. For this we have consistently opted for the masculine 'He', in keeping with the Gurus' own usage and their preference for masculine epithets like 'Lord' or 'Master'. We have similarly preferred the lower case masculine 'he' to refer to the guru. But we have felt less constrained where human subjects are concerned. While not seeking to deliberately substitute a 'she' where the original has an unambiguous 'he', we have adopted a deliberate strategy of trying to be as gender-inclusive as possible, typically through preferring a gender-neutral 'they' where the original uses a singular masculine 'he' when addressing the generic human condition.

Finally, like all honest translators before us, we must conclude by acknowledging that we have been engaged in a task impossible to achieve perfectly. This realization has to be particularly strongly felt when approaching living sacred texts of this power with equipment that is never quite adequate, whether in the technical terms of linguistic or literary gifts or in the grander dimensions of insight and understanding. But if in spite of its necessary imperfections our undertaking helps bring its readers to an enhanced appreciation of the teachings of the Sikh Gurus it will have fully succeeded in its purpose.

1

JAPJI

Guru Nanak's *Japji* is, without question, the greatest of all the many compositions which are contained in the Sikh scriptures. This special status is reflected in the honorific -ji which is commonly added to the name *Jap* or 'Recitation'. It is printed at the beginning of the Adi Granth, on pp. 1–8. It also appears at the beginning of private prayer books, since it is prescribed for daily recitation by all devout Sikhs in the early morning (*amrit vela*).

As its title implies, the *Japji* is composed for recitation as a litany, and it is thus rather different in character from the bulk of the contents of the Adi Granth, which are primarily composed for singing and are arranged under the various ragas. It is similar to many of Guru Nanak's other compositions in its language, which is essentially a mixture of Old Punjabi and Old Hindi with a variety of technical terms from Sanskrit and Persian. But it is highly distinctive in style. Like most litanies, the *Japji* makes great use of the rhetorical device of anaphora, the repetition of the same word or phrase at the beginning of several successive lines, which are themselves often composed of densely packed sequences of nouns and names.

But in deliberate counterpoint to this sameness, great use is also made of a variety of formal structures. Instead of the regular organized stanzas used in most of the Gurus' longer poems, like *Asa ki Var*, the *Japji* is designed with numerous inbuilt changes of pace.

Different metres and rhyming patterns are used in different stanzas
(*pauri*), short stanzas alternate with much longer ones, and several
sets of stanzas are marked by the repetition of their closing verses at
the end of each. Since its unique form is so important to the expansion of consciousness which this magnificent litany is so wonder-
fully designed to produce, a deliberate attempt has been made to
reproduce as many of its features as possible in the translation, with
the usual exception of the rhymes which are so very difficult to
reproduce at all naturally in English.

Clearly the work of Guru Nanak's maturity, the *Japji* brings
together all the key themes explored in the Sikh scriptures around
its central core of the praise of the unknowable divinity in uniquely
magnificent terms. It is consequently in itself a profound exercise in
the spiritual discipline of which the Gurus continually speak, culminating in the final stanzas' succinct description of the several
mystical realms (*khand*), to whose elucidation much subsequent
effort has been given.

The opening credal statement or *Mul Mantar* is followed by an
introductory *shalok* and thirty-eight stanzas. Their content and
formal arrangement may be summarized as follows:

1. The need to follow the divine will and command (*hukam*).
2. List of the universal operations of the divine command.
3. List of those who sing praises of God, the indescribable One.
4. Praise of God and the Name.
5. Praise of the divine manifestations (*refrain A: invocation to the guru*).
6. Praise of the guru's teachings (*refrain A*).
7. Impossibility of human description of the divine.
8–11. Lists of the results of listening to the Name (*refrain B: the blessings of the Name*).
12–15. Lists of the results of acceptance (*refrain C: how the Name is to be known through acceptance*).
16. Praise of the saints and of the divine power (*refrain D: the Formless One is beyond description*).
17. List of the countless types of good people (*refrain D*).
18. List of the countless types of bad people (*refrain D*).
19. List of the attributes of the unknowable divinity (*refrain D*).

20. The power of the Name to save, and the responsibility of man for actions.
21. Unknowability of the moment of creation.
22. How the scriptures are unable to describe creation.
23. How all praise is inadequate, and all worldly wealth inferior to devotion.
24. How God surpasses all efforts to praise Him.
25. The infinite bounty of God.
26. List of God's attributes, far beyond the ability of any to describe them.
27. Great hymn to all those who sing to the Lord.
28. Attributes of the true yogi (*refrain E: all hail to the Primal Being!*).
29–31. Celebration of the universal power of the divine (*refrain E*).
32. Inability of the human tongue to describe Him.
33. How all that happens is by the divine will.
34. The realm of righteous action.
35–6. The realm of wisdom.
37. The realm of action, and the realm of truth.
38. Summary of the discipline needed for spiritual transformation by divine favour.

The last stanza is followed by a concluding *shalok* which is not part of the numbered sequence.

One, Manifest as Word, True of Name, Creative Being, Without Fear, Without Enmity, Whose Form is Infinite, Unborn, Self-Existent, through the grace of the guru.

Repeat

True in the beginning, True before time began,
He is True, Nanak, and ever will be True.

1

No idea of Him can be conceived through thousands of thoughts,[1]
Ultimate silence evades the most deep meditation.
To heap up the wealth of the world does not lessen man's hunger,
And multiple cleverness will not assist us hereafter.
Nanak says: How to be cleared? How to break down the wall of the
   ego? –
Follow His will and command, from the first written out.[2]

2

By the command,[3] forms are produced,
But the command cannot be defined.
By the command, creatures exist,
By the command, greatness is gained.
By the command, men are made high and made low,
By the command, sorrows and joys are received.
By the command, some are granted His favour,
By the command, some must forever revolve.
All are within the command,
Outside of it no one can live.
Nanak, to grasp the command
Is to renounce ego-sense.

3

Some sing of His power, for they have the power,
Some sing of His bounty, for they know its signs.
Some sing of His virtues, greatness and acts,
Some sing of His knowledge, so hard to imagine.

Some sing of His making, the body, then dust,
Some sing of His taking, and giving back life.
Some sing that He seems and appears far away,
Some sing that He sees all, present and here.
In His description, no shortfall is found
As millions try over and over again.
He never stops giving, the takers get tired,
Throughout all the ages, they feed and they feed.
Through the command, it is the command that lays out the way.
Nanak, free from all care He rejoices.

4

The Lord is True, and True in Name,
Whose speech is love that has no limit.
They beg and ask, 'O give, O give'
The Giver then bestows His bounty.
What can be offered in return
To gain the prospect of His court?
What words to be expressed are there,
To cause Him to bestow His love?
Before the dawn[4] reflect upon
The greatness of the Name that's True.
Through deeds we've done we get this garment,[5]
Through grace we reach salvation's gate.
Nanak, it must be realized
That of Himself He's All and True.

5

He cannot be established, nor can He be made,
Of Himself He exists, quite free from all stain.
Through serving Him truly, great honour is found,
O Nanak, sing praise of the store of all virtue.
Sing praises and listen, feel love in your heart,
Let sorrow be banished and joy take its place.
Through the guru the Word and its wisdom are shown
Through the guru awareness of immanence.
The guru is Shiv, he is Vishnu and Brahma

The guru is Parvati, known as the Mother.
If I knew Him, I still could not say what He's like,
His description is something that cannot be told.
    O guru, teach me only this:
    Let me not forget
    The One who gives to all.

6

His pleasure is my pilgrimage,[6]
What use is bathing otherwise?
One lesson from the guru fills
The mind that hears with precious gems.
    O guru, teach me only this:
    Let me not forget
    The One who gives to all.

7

If one could live for all four ages,
Or even ten times longer still,
If one were known in all nine realms,
Enjoying universal admiration,
If one acquired great reputation,
Great fame and glory in the world –
Yet who would pay the slightest notice,
Without that look of favour from Him?
To worms that wretch would be a worm,
Whom even sinners would condemn.
To those who lack and those who have them,
O Nanak, virtues come from Him.
On Him, though, virtue cannot be
Conferred by anyone that's here.

8

Through hearing It:[7] the Siddhs and Pirs and sages.
Through hearing It: the earth and bull and heaven.
Through hearing It: the zones and worlds and underworlds.

Through hearing It: death has no power to menace.
   Nanak, the saints gain bliss forever,
   Through hearing It: the end of pain and sin.

9

Through hearing It: Isar, Brahma, Indra.
Through hearing It: wicked mouths are filled with praise.
Through hearing It: yoga and the body's secrets.
Through hearing It: Shastras, Smritis, Vedas.
   Nanak, the saints gain bliss forever,
   Through hearing It: the end of pain and sin.

10

Through hearing It: truth, contentment, wisdom.
Through hearing It: bathing in all sixty-eight.[8]
Through hearing It: recitation brings great honour.
Through hearing It: attention comes quite easily.[9]
   Nanak, the saints gain bliss forever,
   Through hearing It: the end of pain and sin.

11

Through hearing It: the pool of virtues' depths.
Through hearing It: the Shaykhs, the Pirs, the kings.
Through hearing It: the blind can find their way.
Through hearing It: the bottomless is plumbed.
   Nanak, the saints gain bliss forever,
   Through hearing It: the end of pain and sin.

12

The state of acceptance[10] is not to be told,
If anyone tries, they will later repent.
With pen on the paper, no hard-thinking writer
Can capture the slightest idea of acceptance.
   Such is the Name which is free from all stain,
   To be known to the mind through acceptance.

13

Through acceptance, awareness envelops the mind.
Through acceptance, the universe comes to be known.
Through acceptance, all slaps on the face[11] are avoided.
Through acceptance, there is no departure with death.
　　Such is the Name which is free from all stain,
　　To be known to the mind through acceptance.

14

Through acceptance, no obstacle stands in our way.
Through acceptance, we're given distinction and honour.
Through acceptance, we keep to the road we should travel.
Through acceptance, right action stays closely connected.
　　Such is the Name which is free from all stain,
　　To be known to the mind through acceptance.

15

Through acceptance, we come to discover the gate of salvation.
Through acceptance, support is provided to us and our kinsfolk.
Through acceptance, the guru is saved, and he saves his disciples.
Through acceptance, O Nanak, none need to keep begging.
　　Such is the Name which is free from all stain,
　　To be known to the mind through acceptance.

16

The saints are approved, the saints are supreme,
The saints receive honour, as they stand in the court.
The saints are exalted, as kings at the gate,
The saints' thoughts are fixed on the guru alone.
Although one may speak and try to describe them,
The works of the Maker cannot be counted.
The Bull[12] that is righteousness, offspring of mercy,
Is tethered in place with the rope of contentment.
If we can see this, we indeed must acknowledge
What the burden must be which lies on the bull.

There are many more worlds beyond earth, then yet more,
What strength must the one who's beneath them possess?
The names of the creatures, their kinds and their colours,
Are all written down by the flow of His pen.
Supposing that someone knew how to record them,
How long an account would then have to be written!
How great is His power, how lovely His beauty!
How great is His bounty, which cannot be priced!
With a single command this vast world was created,
On which hundreds and thousands of currents[13] emerged.
    To describe You is beyond me,
    Your quite unworthy offering.
    That deed is good which pleases You,
    O Formless One, secure forever.

17

Countless the prayers, and countless the reverence,
Countless the worship, and countless the penance,
Countless the scriptures and readers of Vedas,
Countless the yogis whose minds are detached,
Countless the saints who think on His virtues,
Countless the pious, and countless the givers,
Countless the heroes who boldly face steel,
Countless the silent absorbed in devotion.
    To describe You is beyond me,
    Your quite unworthy offering.
    That deed is good which pleases You,
    O Formless One, secure forever.

18

Countless the fools who are totally blind,
Countless the thieves who live off their crimes,
Countless the tyrants who issue commands,
Countless the cut-throats who murder and kill,
Countless the sinners who sin till they die,
Countless the liars who go round in lies,
Countless the outcastes who eat and speak filth,

Countless the slanderers burdened by spite.
  The lowly Nanak says: I am
  Your quite unworthy offering.
  That deed is good which pleases You,
  O Formless One, secure forever.

19

Countless Your titles, and countless Your places,
Countless and far beyond reach Your domains.
Calling them countless increases the burden.[14]
Through words comes the Name, through words come the praises,
Through words come both wisdom and songs to Your virtues.
Through words come reciting and writing the Word,
Through words on the forehead, our fate is described.
  The Writer has no words upon Him,
  As He commands, so they receive.
  His Name is great, as is creation.
  There is no place without the Name.
  To describe You is beyond me,
  Your quite unworthy offering.
  That deed is good which pleases You,
  O Formless One, secure forever.

20

When dust falls on our limbs and bodies
It can be washed away with water.
When urine makes a garment foul
It can be washed away with soap.
The colour of the Name will clean
The mind that is befouled by sins.
The record of your deeds goes with you,
'Saint' and 'sinner' aren't just names.
It's you who sow, and you who reap,
O Nanak, birth and death are as decreed.

21

Hardly the tiniest grain's worth of honour
Comes through bathing, austerity, pity and charity.
Hearing, acceptance,[15] love in the heart
Show the place for true bathing and cleansing within.
 All virtues are Yours, in me there are none.
 Without practising virtue, there is no devotion.
 I salute You, Creator, the World and the Word,
 The True and the Lovely, delight of my heart!
What was the time, what was the hour?
What was the date by moon and by sun?[16]
What was the month, what was the season?
When did the world come into being?
The time was not found by the Pandits,
For it to be in the Puranas.
The hour was not found by the Qazis,
For the Koran to record it.
The date is unknown to the yogis,
None know the season or month.
The One who created this world,
The Creator alone knows the time.
 How can I speak, how can I praise?
 How can I tell, how can I know?
 Plenty pretend they can tell,
 Nanak, they claim to be smart.
 Great is the Lord, great is His Name
 Whatever He does come to pass.

22

 Lower worlds below each other,
 Heavens thousand-fold above:
 That search for limits is exhausting
 Is the Vedas' sole conclusion.
 All Puranas and the scriptures
 Agree there is one basic source.
 It would be written if they could,
 But it can't be written down.

Nanak, simply call Him great,
It's He who knows how great He is.

23

The praises which praisers express
Do not gain them sufficient awareness.
Once rivers and channels flow into the sea
They no longer remain distinct.
Rulers and kings may possess
Oceans and mountains of wealth,
But are less than the tiniest ant
In whose mind He is never forgotten.

24

There's no end to His praise, no end to its telling,
There's no end to His works, no end to His giving.
There's no end to His seeing, no end to His hearing,
There's no end that is known to what's in His mind.
There's no end that is known to the world that He made,
There's no end that is known to His limits.
Though many may yearn to determine them,
His boundaries cannot be found.
None can discover this limit,
Which always exceeds its description.
Great is the Lord, and high is His place
And higher than high is His Name.
Only if we were as high as He is
Could we hope to determine His height.
Only to Him can His greatness be known,
Nanak, the glance of His grace is our gift.

25

Great is His kindness, which cannot be written,
Great is the Giver, who has no grain of greed.
So many, the crowds of the heroes who beg,
So many, their numbers cannot be reckoned.

So many are wasted and ruin their gifts,
So many keep getting, but deny they've received.
So many are fools who just keep on consuming,
So many keep suffering sorrow and hunger.
These also are gifts which You give us.
Your will determines release from our bondage,
No one else has a say about this.
Any loud-mouth who speaks up should know
He'll be shamed and his face will be slapped.
The Knower and Giver are one and the same,
Though this is acknowledged by few.
Those granted the gift of offering praise,
Nanak says, will be kings over kings.

26

Priceless Your virtues, priceless Your dealings,
Priceless Your traders, priceless Your treasures,
Priceless Your comers, priceless Your buyers,
Priceless Your lovers, priceless Your mergers,
Priceless Your justice, priceless Your court,
Priceless Your balance, priceless Your weights,
Priceless Your bounty, priceless Your seal,
Priceless Your mercy, priceless Your order.
Priceless, so priceless, You cannot be told,
Though the effort absorbs us in love.
　　The Vedas, Puranas and scriptures all tell,
　　The commentaries and the great scholars all tell,
　　The Brahmas all tell, and the Indras all tell,
　　The Gopis all tell, the Govindas tell too,
　　The Isars all tell, and so too do the Siddhs,
　　The numbers created of Buddhas all tell,
　　The demons all tell, and so too do the gods,
　　The sages all tell, and so too do the yogis.
　　So many are telling and trying to tell,
　　So many while telling rise up and depart.
　　You could make many more than all these,
He's as great as He chooses to be,
As is known to the True One Himself.

Any loud-mouth who dares to describe Him,
Should be branded 'most stupid of fools'.

27

How great is that gate,[17] and how great is that house,
Where You sit and take care of all things!
So many instruments, so many players,
So many ragas[18] and so many singers!
To You sing the wind and the water and fire,
To You sings the Judge[19] at the gate,
To You sing the writers called Chitra and Gupta,
Whose record assists the Judge to decide.
To You sing too Isar and Brahma, adorned
In their glory along with the goddess.
To You sing too Indras enthroned on their seats
Along with the gods at the gate.
To You sing the Siddhs in profound meditation,
To You sing the saints in their deep contemplation.
To You sing the true, the content and the celibate,
To You sing the warriors, the fiercest of heroes,
To You sing the pandits and greatest of rishis,
Reciting the Vedas throughout all the ages,
To You sing the fair ones who capture the heart
In heaven, on earth, and down in the underworld.
To You sing the jewels which You have created
Along with the sixty-eight places of bathing.
To You sing the fighters whose strength is heroic,
To You sing the quadruple orders of being,[20]
To You sing the realms and the spheres and the worlds,
Which You have created and You have preserved.
To You sing all those in whom You delight,
The saints who are steeped in the joy of Your love.
To You sing so many I cannot remember,
Says Nanak, how can I conceive them?
    It is He, it is He who always is True,
    The Lord who is True, and True is His Name.
    He is and He will be, never departing,
    The One who created the whole of creation.

He fashioned the spectacle this world presents
In its multiple colours and various kinds.
He makes and He watches what He has created
As fully accords with His infinite greatness.
He always will act in the way that He pleases,
No order can ever be issued to rule Him.
It is He who is sovereign, the king of all kings,
Nanak says, to whose pleasure all life must be subject.

28

Let contentment be your earrings, modesty your pouch,
Let meditation be the ashes smeared upon you.
With fear of death as cloak to wrap your virgin body
Make faith your yoga, let it be the staff you wield.
With all humanity belonging to your order[21]
Let conquest of the mind bring conquest of the world.
  All hail, all hail to Him,
  The primal, untouched, unstarted, unchanging,
  Throughout all the ages the same!

29

The food of wisdom is dispensed by mercy,
The mystic music sounds in every heart.
God is the lord who has complete control,
Beyond all riches and all magic powers.
Union and separation work in rhythm,
And all receive the fortune which is written.
  All hail, all hail to Him,
  The primal, untouched, unstarted, unchanging,
  Throughout all the ages the same!

30

One the mother, made according to design,
Three the disciples who meet with acceptance:
Creator, provider, and holder of court,[22]
Each set to work as He commands and wills,

Who sees, unseen, how wonderful this is!
 All hail, all hail to Him,
  The primal, untouched, unstarted, unchanging,
  Throughout all the ages the same!

31

His seat and His stores are in every world,
Whatever is found there was placed all at once.
The Creator first made, and then He beholds,
Nanak, the works of the True One are true.
 All hail, all hail to Him,
  The primal, untouched, unstarted, unchanging,
  Throughout all the ages the same!

32

If this one tongue became a hundred thousand,
If they in turn were multiplied by twenty,
They would take a hundred thousand times
To praise the one Name of the Lord.
This is the way to climb the stairs
That lead to union with Him.
By hearing such accounts of heaven
The humblest worms are roused to act.
Through grace alone is He attained,
Not through those liars' idle boasts.

33

Saying and silence are not in our power,
Begging and giving are not in our power,
Living and dying are not in our power.
The gaining of riches and empire, which causes
Such mental distraction, is not in our power.
True awareness and wisdom are not in our power,
Escape from the world is not in our power.
Power rests with the One who makes and who watches –
Nanak, the high and the low are as nothing before Him.

34

Nights, seasons, weekdays, lunar dates,
Winds, water, fire and lower worlds,
And in the midst of these lies earth,
Fixed as the place of righteous action,[23]
Containing different kinds of creatures,
Whose names are many and untold.
They are judged according to their deeds,
As He is true, so is His court.
Approved, the saints are glorified,
For they receive His mark of grace.
There bad and good will stand revealed,
On going there, this will be known.

35

Such is the realm of righteous action,
Now to describe the realm of wisdom:
So many winds and fires and waters,
So many Krishnas and Maheshes,
So many Brahmas are created,
Of varied shapes and forms and colours!
So many peaks and earths to act in,
So many Dhruvs to give instruction,
So many Indras, moons and suns,
So many spheres there are and countries!
So many Buddhas, Siddhs and Naths,
So many goddesses incarnate,
So many demons, gods and sages,
So many jewel-bearing oceans!
So many kinds of life and language,
So many emperors and kings,
So many mystics and attendants!
O Nanak, there's no end, no end.

36

In that realm, wisdom reigns supreme
With music, song, delight and joy.
   The realm of bliss[24] is forged so finely
   That beauty is its only language.
   It cannot be described at all,
   Whoever tries must soon repent.
   Forged here are wisdom and perception,
   The insight of the Siddhs and sages.

37

It's power and nothing else which is
The language of the realm of action.
Its warriors, those mighty heroes,
Are strengthened by the force of Ram,[25]
In glory there are many Sitas,
Whose beauty cannot be described.
Those in whose minds Ram's Name resides
Can neither die nor be deceived.
   There many worlds of saints rejoice
   To have the True One in their hearts.
   The realm of truth is where the Formless
   Resides and, watching all creation,
   Makes happy by a look of favour.
These universes, realms and spheres
Surpass all efforts to describe them.
There worlds on worlds and countless forms
All operate by His command.
He watches, pleased as He regards them.
Nanak says: To tell of this is hard as eating iron.

38

With restraint as the furnace, persistence as goldsmith,
With awareness as anvil, true knowledge as hammer,
With fear as the bellows, with penance as burner,
In love as the vessel, the Name is dissolved,
Producing the Word in the mint that is true.
    This is what those who are favoured perform,
    Blessed by His glance of kindness and grace.

*

Air is the guru and water the father, great earth is the mother,
Day and night are the nurses who dandle the world.
In the court Death recites all our deeds, good and bad,
Which decide who is close, who is far from the Presence.
    Some think on the Name and depart having worked well,
    How bright are their faces, with them how many are freed![26]

2

IMPERMANENCE

The Gift and Curse of Time

If the recurrent theme of Guru Nanak's *Japji* is to unite the mind separated from its divine source through constant remembrance of the Name, this is because the element in which separation and unification takes place is time. Not surprisingly, therefore, the theme of time is one of the most pervasive in Sikh scripture. However, the Gurus do not specifically treat time as an entity distinct from the phenomenal world and from existent being, primarily because time is simultaneously subjective and objective.

Ordinarily we tend to think of time as a static grid or a screen on which subjects appear to move between set coordinates, e.g. from past to future. From this dualistic perspective, time is never 'my time', but always out there, someone else's time. To collapse this dualism Guru Nanak adopts the well-rehearsed Indian strategy of shrinking the entire passage of human life into a single night, depicting the night's progression in terms of infancy, childhood, youth and old age (2.1, 2.2, 2.8). To the person who refuses to confront the true nature of time as impermanent here and now ('one dies, but not me, not yet'), the Gurus project the intolerable face of time as one's own mortality that is always already there and cannot be deferred. Through this depiction one is existentially confronted with the presence of death here and now. Reversing our normal understanding, the Gurus show how, from the perspective of impermanence, the usual secure optimism of daylight and the waking state turn out to be illusions, whereas night and the dreaming state are better indicators of reality.

The nature of time as the ultimate equalizer of fortunes is evident in other hymns which show that if one rises, one must ultimately fall, irrespective of whether that fall happens in one's own lifetime, as shown by the plight of the princesses who fell victim to Babur's marauding army (2.5), or whether it occurs after one's life has been lived, portrayed below in Shaykh Farid's austere verse:

> Umbrella-shaded kings, whose praise
> Their bards to drum-beats cried,
> Are gone to slumber in their graves,
> With orphans at their side.
> Shalok Farid 45, p. 1380

Time is, however, nothing if not paradoxical. According to the Gurus, it is neither real nor illusory, yet both; neither subjective nor objective, yet both. On the one hand, time is the matrix in which the self is trapped. Having forgotten its true nature as impermanent and becoming attached to worldly projects, beauty, youth and wealth, it suffers and grieves when these things are lost (2.6, 2.7). On the other hand, given that the locus of one's existence in time is the body, time is a gift. Likening the temporal body to a full-blooded mare, the Guru urges man to saddle up and to ride life in order to cross the sea of existence (2.9).

While ordinarily people lament the passing of time, grieving for things lost (2.10), and suffering pain when attachments are broken (2.11), the Guru teaches that attachment and suffering result only from our habitual obstruction of the natural flow of time. By accepting time's impermanence as our own essence and seeing every attempt to control time as ultimately illusory like the waves of the sea, which are here one moment, gone the next, one can be released from suffering (2.6). By cultivating mindfulness of the Name, one can learn to renounce self-attachment as the insidious obstacle to the flow of time (2.11). With the obstruction removed the mind is freed from its self-imposed bindings, from its immersion in the cycle of birth and death, and from the anxiety of being born into one life-form after another (2.4).

The leading ideas in the hymns selected under the theme of impermanence can be summarized as follows:

2.1　Man's life condensed into the four watches of night: (1) in the womb, mind is attached to the Name; (2) in early infancy, mind starts to separate by creating a sense of other; (3) during youth and middle age, mind is engrossed in worldly projects; (4) with the onset of old age and death, mind is helpless and forlorn.

2.2　Ten stages of life representing the speed of time's passage.

2.3　Grief as the mark of impermanence contains its own cure.

2.4　Transmigration and the cycle of births and deaths.

2.5　The reality of impermanence manifested in a single lifetime's rise and fall.

2.6　The illusory, because transient, nature of human relationships.

2.7　The falseness of worldly love.

2.8　The momentariness of man's stay in this world.

2.9　The body as a vehicle for traversing the sea of existence: time as gift.

2.10　Life's transience likened to a woman's stay in her parental home.

2.11　The solution for the extreme sufferings and anxieties of time is remembrance of the Name.

(2.1)[1]

In the night's first watch, my trader friend,
    You were posted to the womb.
Where upside down, my trader friend,
    Your thoughts and prayers were fixed on God.
As upside down you prayed to Him,
    Your devotion was complete.
You came here quite convention-free
    And naked you will leave the world.
Each helpless creature must endure
    The written fate its forehead bears.
Say, Nanak: In the night's first watch, my soul,
    You were posted to the womb.

In the night's next watch, my trader friend,
    The focus of your mind was lost.
They played with you, my trader friend,
    Like Krishna in Yasodha's house
Each took their turn to play with you:
    Your mother said, 'This child is mine.'
Remember, thick unseeing mind,
    You will have nothing at the last,
So let this wisdom fill your thoughts
    Which know not Him who fashioned you.
Say, Nanak; In the night's next watch, my soul,
    The focus of your mind was lost.

In the night's third watch, my trader friend,
    Your thoughts were fixed on wealth and looks.
You quite forgot, my trader friend,
    The Name which saves you from your bonds.
Here all those who forget the Name
    Must live distracted by the world.
Obsessed with wealth and drunk on looks,
    You've wasted this whole life of yours.
You've done no trade in righteousness
    And have not made good deeds your friends.
Say, Nanak: In the night's third watch, my soul,
    Your thoughts were fixed on wealth and looks.

In the night's fourth watch, my trader friend,
    The reaper comes into the field.
None is informed, my trader friend,
    When death will come to send them off.
When death will come to send them off
    Is known to God and no one else.
This lamentation is quite false
    The dead one is their kin no more.
And what you get is only that
    On which you fastened so much love
Say, Nanak: In the night's fourth watch, my soul,
    The reaper harvested the field.
                      Srirag M1 Pahare 1, p. 74

(2.2)

The first fastens in love on the breast and its milk,
The second takes in the father and mother.
The third distinguishes sisters and brothers,
The fourth develops a fondness for play.
The fifth is devoted to eating and drinking,
The sixth is for sex with no thought of caste.
The seventh is setting up home with a partner,
The eighth is for rage as the body grows weak.
The ninth sees shortness of breath and white hair,
The tenth is for burning till ashes are left.
As the funeral party utters laments,
The soul flies away and asks where to go.
Life came and is gone and so too has the fame,
Leaving only the offerings for crows to be called to.
Nanak, the love of the self-led is blind,
Without the true guru the world drowns in darkness.
                      Majh ki Var, M1 1.2, p. 137

(2.3)

In grief we're born, in grief we die,
    In grief the world transacts its tasks.
It's grief that will be talked of there,

As all recite their sufferings.
Unwrapping grief's tight packages
   Does not let any joy emerge.
In grief his spirit was consumed,
   Aggrieved he wept and went away.
But, Nanak, happy is the state
   Of mind and body steeped in praise.
They may be killed by fires of grief,
   And yet grief is their remedy.
            Sarang ki Var, M1 8.1, p. 1240

(2.4)

You're often born as worm or moth,
As elephant or fish or deer.
You're often born as bird or snake,
As horse, or ox that's yoked.

R.   So meet the world's Lord, now's the time,
      Since you have found this form at last.

You're often born as rock or crag,
You're often taken in the womb.
You're often born as tree or plant
To make up eighty-four lakh[2] births.

This human birth comes through the saints,
Perform His service, say His Name.
Renounce false arrogance and pride,
Be dead in life, gain honour there.

The past is Yours, the future too,
For no one else has any power
We meet You only if You will
O Nanak, sing the praise of God.
            Gauri Guareri M5 3, p. 176

(2.5)[3]

The ladies' hair once parted with vermilion
Is scissored off from heads now covered with the dust,

They have nowhere to sit who once had palaces.

R. Hail, First Being, hail!
    Your limits are unreached, You watch these changing scenes.

Beside them at their weddings how fine their grooms appeared,
Adorned with ivory they came in palanquins
With water sprinkled on them and shining fans to hand.

They once were offered gold each time they stood or sat,
They lay about and nibbled coconuts and dates,
Their strings of pearls are broken from necks that now bear chains.

The wealth and looks they flaunted have become their foes,
Dishonoured now by soldiers they are taken off.
As He decides, He gives the glory and the pain.

Why should we suffer pain if first we think of Him?
The princes lost in luxury forgot themselves,
But once they heard of Babur they could not even eat.

Some women cannot pray, for some their worship's gone
The Hindus have no squares, no baths or forehead-marks
They cannot call on Allah who never thought of Ram.

Some come back home, some ask if all is well,
For some it is decided that they shall sit and weep.
What pleases Him must happen, Nanak, what is man?

Asa M1 A11, p. 417

(2.6)

R. Relationships are just for life
    With parents, siblings, children, kin or wife.

The moment that you cease to breathe, they shout
That you're a ghost who must be driven out.

The world like a mirage around us waves
Recite with love the Name of God which saves.

Devgandhari M9 2, p. 536

(2.7)

R.   In this world love is false, I see,
       All chase their own delight, both spouse and friend.

'You're mine' all say to those they think they love,
It's strange these ties are broken in the end.

This stupid mind still does not get my point –
The world-sea's only crossed by praising God.

Devgandhari M9 3, p. 536

(2.8)

A momentary guest, man comes to sort things out.[4]
The fool, not understanding, is trapped by worldly greed
Till, seized by wretched death, he repents when he departs.

R.   You're blind, you fool, yet sit right on the edge,
       If former deeds allow it, do what the guru says.

The reaper cuts both ripe and unripe when he comes,
He makes his preparations, picking up his scythe,
For once the farmer orders, the crop is cut and weighed.

The first watch[5] goes on busyness, the next in sleep,
The third in idle talk, and in the fourth dawn breaks,
The Lord who gave us life is never thought of once.

I am devoted to the company of saints,
Through whom I'm made aware and can come close to Him,
The all-wise Being who is Nanak's inner guide.

Srirag M5 74, p. 43

(2.9)[6]

This body's a mare which is fashioned by God,
How blessed is this human existence which virtue bestows!
Human birth is obtained through great virtue, this body is made of
    fine gold,
Through the guru its colour is scarlet, the Name ever dyes it afresh.
The body which calls upon God is adorned by the Name,

Obtained by great luck with the Name as its helper, Nanak, it's
fashioned by God.

I saddle the body with good thoughts of Him,
Upon it I'm able to cross this laborious world-sea.
The world-sea has so many waves, and only the guru can get one
across,
The lucky will go in His boat, which is steered with the Word by
the guru.
Dyed daily in God and reaching to God, God's lover sings praises of
Him,
The ultimate state is arrived at by Nanak, God's state is sublime and
is good.

The guru makes wisdom the bit in my mouth,
He lays on the whip of God's love to my body.
Applying the whip of God's love to the body brings victory over the
mind,
The untrained is trained and the Word is discovered, the nectar is
drunk
When the ears hear the Word of the guru, the mare is dyed in the
Lord,
The way is so long and so toilsome, but Nanak has got to the end.

This body's a mare which is fashioned by God,
How blessed is the mare by which the Lord God is remembered!
Bravo for the mare by which He's remembered, bred from our
former good deeds!
This mare gets us over the world-sea, to reach the most Blissful Lord
through the guru.
The Lord who is perfect has set up the wedding, the groom has the
saints in his party,
Nanak the humble has God as his groom, the saints come to sing
songs of joy.

Vadhans M4 Ghorian 1, p. 575

(2.10)

These riches, youth and flowers are but passing guests,
Which like the lotus-petals bloom to drift away.

R.   Enjoy your fun while you are young and fair
     Your days are few and soon your garb grows old.

My handsome friends have gone to slumber in the grave,
I too would go who grieve and softly weep for them.

Fair maiden, have these ears of yours not heard the news?
You can't stay here, but must go to your in-laws' house.

You'd think a burglar boldly robbed her parents' home
And stole her virtues, so she's packed her faults instead.

                                        Srirag M1 24, p. 23

(2.11)

When problems are too great, when no one offers help,
When friends turn into foes, when relatives go off,
When all support is lost, when no help's at hand,
Remembrance of the Lord protects from every harm.

R.   He is the power of the powerless,
     He does not come or go, forever He remains.
     Know through the guru that He is Truth.

When weakness comes from hunger or from poverty,
When there's no money and there's no one to provide,
When aims do not succeed and nothing can get done,
Remembrance of the Lord gives kingship that remains.

When worries overwhelm and when the body's ill,
When family concerns rouse feelings good and bad,
When restlessness prevents a moment of repose,
Remembrance of the Lord produces peace and calm.

Though lust and anger grip, with greed and worldly love,
Though these four evils make man a demon to be killed,
Though scriptures, hymns and sacred verse remain unheard,
Remembrance of the Lord has instant power to save.

Though Vedas, Shastras, Smritis may be learnt by heart,
Though as a yogi pilgrimages are performed,
Though worship and the six-fold rites are doubly done,
Yet not to love the Lord ensures despatch to hell.

Though lands and lordships and fine pleasures are enjoyed,
Though gardens may be owned, to issue proud commands,
Though parties may be held upon a lavish scale,
But not to think of God brings rebirth as a snake.

Though wealth and good behaviour may confer good name,
Though family and friends and parents may be loved,
Though well-armed guards may be there to salute and cheer,
But not to think of God ensures the worst of hells.

Though bodies may be healthy and hearts be free from pain,
Though death may be forgotten in pleasures night and day,
Though great possessions bring a freedom from all care,
But not to think of God empowers death to strike.

When God is kind, the company of saints is found,
Love for the Lord will grow, the closer it is kept,
There is no place but Him, the Lord of both the worlds,
O Nanak, when the guru's pleased, the True Name is obtained.

Srirag M5 A1, p. 70

3

ASA KI VAR

The var is one of the main narrative forms of Panjabi poetry. Loosely corresponding to the English ballad, it consists of a set of stanzas called pauri or 'step', each made up of a set of rhyming verses. While the traditional var composed by the minstrels deals with the battles of tribal chiefs and praise of their bravery, Guru Nanak converted the form to the very different purpose of hymning the greatness of God and the divine organization of the world. Of his three compositions in this genre in the ragas of Majh, Asa and Malhar, which were designed to be performed to the familiar patterns of traditional ballads, by far the best-known is this 'Ballad in Asa' or Asa ki Var (in modern Panjabi Asa di Var), which appears on pp. 462–74 of the Adi Granth. It has an important place in gurdwara ritual, where it is regularly sung in the early morning performances.

In the Adi Granth, the text of Asa ki Var is headed 'Asa M1, Var with shaloks also written by M1, to the tune of Asraj the Maimed'. In Guru Arjan's edition of the Var, each stanza is preceded by two or more shaloks of more or less relevance to the theme of the following pauri. Most of these 59 shaloks are also by Guru Nanak but 15 are by his immediate successor Guru Angad. So Guru Nanak's first pauri, which praises the majesty of God and His creation, is preceded in the Adi Granth by three shaloks in praise of the guru through whom that majesty is known. The first shalok by Guru Nanak provides the formal model for the second by Guru Angad, while the third shalok by Guru Nanak uses a strikingly different image to address the same theme:

Shalok M1

I'm devoted to the guru a hundred times a day,
Who in making men and gods suffered no delay.

M2

Let a hundred moons arise, a thousand suns, I say:
Their light, without the guru, cannot drive the dark away.

M1

They forget the guru but think themselves alert,
They're like a seedless sesame in an empty field.
Abandoned there to stand for anyone to claim,
Their outward fruit and bloom masking inner ash.

1

Alone You made Yourself, alone You made Your name
You made creation next, You sit to watch its play.
Both Giver and Creator, as You please You give.
All-knower who grants and takes the body and the soul,
You sit to watch its play.

This sustained interplay between each stanza and the *shaloks* placed before it does indeed add a notable dialectic richness, but it can also make it difficult for those not imbued with the text through constant familiarity to grasp the tightly organized underlying structure of Guru Nanak's original composition. While some of the *shaloks* added to *Asa ki Var* will be found separately under other headings in this book, only the stanzas of the *var* are accordingly translated below. Since the expression is often condensed, a very schematic summary of their content may be supplied to demonstrate the extraordinary skill with which the many aspects of the laws of human salvation are brought together for serial treatment:

1. The majesty of God and His control of His creation.
2. The fate of humanity and their subjection to judgement by Death.
3. The fate of the worldly whose birth has been wasted.
4. How the guru offers the possibility of access to the truth.
5. The salvific power of God's Name for those who live properly.
6. The necessity of the guru if God is to be found.
7. Praise of those contented with God's bounty.
8. God's establishment of truth and how the guru can lead to truth.
9. Contrast between God's humble worshippers and the arrogant.
10. Prayer to follow in the footsteps of those who truly serve Him.
11. How God chooses some and not others for access to Him through the guru.
12. Contrast between simple goodness and the deceit of learning.
13. How the guru is a boat which brings those who realize safely to shore.
14. How the body must be left after death and the prospect of hell looms.
15. God's loyal servants and their reward.
16. God's oversight of the world and His capacity to reduce kings to beggary.
17. How the great enjoy their luxury in the world but forget death.
18. Praise to the guru through whom true greatness is granted.
19. The need to acknowledge one's weakness and not to condemn others.
20. How God watches the world whose creatures must take responsibility.
21. How the game of life should be played.
22. A good servant does not try to set up as an equal to the Master.
23. God's infinite power contrasted with human riches.
24. The impossibility of describing God's greatness and omnipotence.

1

Alone You made Yourself, alone You made Your Name,
You made creation next, You sit to watch its play.
Both Giver and Creator, as You please You give,
All-knower who grants and takes the body and the soul,[1]
You sit to watch its play.

2

Once creatures were made, Lord Death[2] was set to judge accounts.
As decided by strict truth, sinners are picked out apart,
The wicked find no place, but are sent black-faced to hell.
Those steeped in Your Name win, while those who trick must lose.
Lord Death was set to judge accounts.

3

Its pleasures done at last, its body turned to ash,
The worldly person's soul is sent with neck in chains,
There to be judged by deeds, with its account explained.
With no escape it's beaten, who hears it when it roars?
Through blinded mind that birth is lost.

4

If You should look with favour, the guru may be found,
Once this soul's roamed many births, the guru's Word's
    proclaimed,
The guru is the greatest giver – hear this, everyone!
His encounter brings the truth when once the self is lost,
The guru who's revealed all truth.

5

Your Name is Formless, through it we need not go to hell,
Body and soul are His, through talking we are lost.
Our own good lies in doing good, in lowliness.
On all who try to put off age, age's marks appear,
None stays here once the measure fills.

6

Without the guru none has found Him, none has found Him,
He put himself in the guru who proclaims Him clear.
The guru's coming brings release, once delusion's lost.
This is the highest wisdom: The mind fixed on the True
Has found the giver, source of life.

7

Well have the contented served who contemplate the truth,
Not setting foot in evil, acting righteously,
Consuming little, breaking off material ties.
You are the greatest giver, who gives increasing gifts
The Great One's found through praising Him.

8

You are the one true Lord, who has established Truth.
Some You grant Truth, and they perform and practise truth
If the guru comes the Truth is found by truth-filled hearts,
But fools don't know the Truth, the self-led waste their birth.
Why did they come into the world?

9

Your worshippers delight You, with praise they deck Your gate,
Where, Nanak, those unfavoured may rush but are shut out.
Some don't know where they're from, in vain they rate themselves.
I'm just a low-caste minstrel (though others think they're great),
Who asks for those who think of You.

10

Give me the dust they tread to smear my forehead with!
Make the unseen your focus, quitting false desires,
For the pattern of our acts determines our reward.
Their dust is granted us if it is so ordained,
But senseless service counts for nought.

11

Those You favoured from the first have attended to the Lord.
Those creatures have no power, You made the varied world
You join some to Yourself, You cause some to be lost.
Through the guru's mercy they know where You proclaim
     Yourself,
And gently absorb Him in the truth.

12

Because the learned sin, should simple saints be beaten?
It is by efforts made that names become renowned.
Avoid those tricks which bring defeat before the court.
When the learned and the simple will have their cases judged
Exploiters will be beaten there.

13

Great guru whose encounter brought the Lord to mind!
With his teaching as their salve, these eyes survey the world.
Attached to the other, some traders left the Lord and roamed.
How few have realized the guru is the boat,
Which delivers those he favours safe.

14

They all must leave their lovely bodies in this world,
The good and ill they each have done, they each shall find,
And they who pleased themselves must tread a narrow path.
As they are stripped and sent to hell, that awful sight,
They must repent the sins they've done.

15

If the Master shows His mercy, He'll get that action done,
That servant whom He makes obey will serve Him well.
Accepted through obedience, he'll find his Master's place,
Doing what the master wants, he'll gain his heart's desire,
And come arrayed before the court.

16

Aware of everyone, He moves all in His gaze,
He gives out every greatness and causes every act.
Great is He and great is His world, where all He sets to work.
But should He look askance, He makes great kings like grass,
To beg at doors and find no alms.

17

With wind-swift horses saddled, in painted palaces,
In chambers and apartments they stretch out at their ease,
Indulging their desires but lost to thoughts of God,
Consuming luxuries but forgetting death.
Old age still comes and youth is lost.

18

Exalt and praise the guru, in whom all glories are!
If God brings us together, those glories are revealed.
Should he so please, they're settled in our hearts
With hand upon our forehead he commands all ills to go
If he so please, all wealth is ours.

19

Most say 'mine, mine!', those who don't are set apart.
As each has done each one must settle their account.
In this world no one stays, why go about in pride?
Make these your rules: Do not say anyone is bad,
And never quarrel with a fool.

20

You it was who made the world and in it set the power.
You watch your world, some pieces home, some still in play.[3]
All who have come will go, each of them in their turn.
How can his breathing creatures not think of the Lord?
They all must undertake to sort their task themselves.

21

Always remember the Lord, whose service brings delight.
When deeds bring their reward, why labour to do ill?
Do nothing bad at all, and take the longer view.
Throw dice that will ensure you do not lose to Him.
Our labour should be done for gain.

22

If servants do their service as their master wills
They win increased respect, and double pay besides.
To try to be their master's equal brings them shame,
The loss of all their pay, and slippers on their face.[4]
All honour should be paid to Him who gives us food
For with the Master prayers, and not commands, avail.

23

God has no limits, Nanak, nor any boundaries,
He causes the creation, then its destruction too.
Some wear necklaces, and some ride many steeds.
He causes, He creates, on whom else should I call?
For He who made this world must keep it in His care.

24

The Great One's greatnesses cannot be described,
Almighty, kind Creator who gives His creatures food.
That task is to be done which from the start He fixed
Nanak, besides the One there is no other place,
He does whatever is His will.

4

MIND, SELF, EGO

Insofar as all is impermanent, likewise mind (*man*) is revealed by the Gurus as the universal basis of experience by individuals. Many terms are used synonymously within Sikh scripture for 'mind', which for the Gurus has two main aspects (4.3). There is, on the one hand, mind in the everyday sense which works under the influence of self-centredness (*haumai*). This aspect of mind-as-ego is subject to space, time and cause and is enticed by form. Mind-as-ego possesses a discriminatory awareness, i.e. a sense of duality which grasps or rejects something external. Fundamentally it is that which falsely posits an 'other' (*duja*) as the basis of external reference and projects itself as the basis of normality and health. From the Gurus' perspective, however, this mind is afflicted by a chronic sickness (4.4, 4.6, 4.12). This is the aspect of mind that plots, calculates, desires, manipulates, flares up in anger and indulges in waves of negative emotions (4.3, 4.5). It needs constantly to assert and confirm its existence by fragmenting, conceptualizing and solidifying experience. Mind-as-ego is described as a stranger to itself, always away from its true home or natural state and consequently subject to continual coming and going through different life-forms (4.6, 4.7).

On the other hand, the same mind, if it renounces ego and orients itself towards the guru's Word, reaches its home ground and is thus liberated from its chronic sickness, and is referred to as the beloved mind (4.3, 4.10). One thing, though, is clear from the Gurus' teaching: liberation is not achieved by annihilating the ego or by simply interiorizing it through excessive discipline (4.8, 4.9). For ego itself is said to contain its own cure (4.3). Because the nature of ego is intrinsically time, the cure involves a spiritual battle with the 'five enemies' of lust, anger, greed, attachment and ego (4.8, 4.13). This is not a battle *against* the world but a battle to exist-in-the-world as radically interconnected to others. At bottom, liberation from ego involves a realization that our singularity is punctured by the presence of other existent beings (not simply human beings), a fact which opens the possibility for an ethics and politics based on mind that is ever in a state of balance (*sahaj*).

Ideas associated in the following compositions with the main themes of mind, self and ego can be summarized as follows:

4.1 Mind is exhorted to give up calculation and cleverness and to contemplate the Name.

4.2 Mind's craving of sensual delights as cause of its pain and separation.

4.3 Dual nature of mind, as ego-centred and non-ego-centred.

4.4 The disease of ego afflicting all existence is removed through the guru's Word.

4.5 All reality and everything we do as conditioned by ego.

4.6 Ego as chronic illness but containing its own cure.

4.7 Metaphysical questions (What? Where? When?) concerning the nature of self.

4.8 Battling with mind as the true work of the spiritual warrior.

4.9 Futility of silencing the mind through force.

4.10 The divine Name and the ego are mutually exclusive.

4.11 Mind's actions are ultimately subject to the divine order.

4.12 The 'five enemies' arise from misuse and under-development of sense perception.

4.13 Attachment as the basis of the other four 'enemies'.

(4.1)

Hear, O mind, this truth I tell:
Seek refuge with the Lord,
Give up your tricks and cleverness
To be absorbed in Him.

Gauri Bavan Akhari M5 50.1, p. 260

(4.2)

Worldly goods are gained through pain,
There's pain when they are lost.
O Nanak, no one's hunger goes
Without the Name that's True.
No beauty can make hunger less,
It grows the more we look.
The joys of sensual delights
Are equalled by their pains.

Malar ki Var, M1 21.2, p. 1287

(4.3)

The mind is an elephant raging in rut
Through the jungle, seduced by the charms of the world.
It roams here and there, under pressure from death,
Through the guru it's able to find its way home.

R.   Without the Word of the guru the mind finds no rest.
     Meditate on the Name of the Lord that is pure
     And renounce the sour flavour of ego.

Explain how this dull-witted mind can be saved,
Without understanding it'll suffer death's pangs.
The merciful Lord brings the guru to some,
For whom death is wiped out as they're driven to Truth.

This mind may be pious and righteous in deed,
The five elements, though, are the place of its birth.[1]
The love of the world makes it greedy and dull.
Through the guru, reciting the Name makes it shine.

Through the guru the mind comes to rest in its home,
Through the guru aware of the triple world's Lord.
Now ascetic or yogi, now sensualist,
Through the guru the mind freely makes out the One.

Renouncing the ego, the mind can detach,
Though desire and duality are in all hearts.
Through the guru it savours the power of the Name,
And then honour is gained at the court of the Lord.

This mind is the king and the hero in war
Through the Name and the guru this mind has no fear.
The five evil passions are slain and subdued,
With ego they're captured and chained in one place.

Through the guru it gives up all other delights
Through the guru the mind to devotion is roused.
The sound that's unstruck makes it ponder the Word,
Made one with the Formless through knowing itself.

This mind is the one that is pure at the court,
When the guru inspires its devotion and love.
Night and day through the guru it praises the Lord,
Who has filled every being since time first began.

Once the power of the Name has enraptured the mind,
Through the guru it knows Him, the source of all tastes.
At the feet of the guru, devotion's aroused:
O Nanak, I'm slave to the slaves of the Lord.

                                        Asa M1 A8, p. 415

(4.4)

That God's in self and self's in God
     The guru has explained.
Through the sweet message of the Word
     Pain stops and ego's killed.

R.   The sicknesses of ego make
     A single pain, seen everywhere.
     Relief's appointed through the Word.

Once they have been assayed by Him
    They are not spiked[2] again.
His look of favour makes them close
    They too are Truth with Him.

Water and air and fire are sick,
    Sick is this sensual world.
Parents and body and wealth are sick,
    Sick is this family.

Brahma and Vishnu and Shiv are sick,
    Sick is the universe.
Those whom the guru shows God's rank
    Are free from this disease.

The rivers, seven seas, nine zones
    And underworlds are sick.
His people, whom His glance preserves,
    Live happy in the Truth.

Sick are ascetics of all kinds,
    Dressed in their orders' robes.
No help can come from holy books
    Which do not know the One.

Sick are the feasters on fine foods,
    Like those who live on roots.
All those who wander from the Name
    Must finally repent.

It is not cured by pilgrimage
    And learning makes things worse.
Duality's a fierce disease
    Which ties us to this world.

Through praise and through the guru's Word
    This illness is removed.
Nanak, His devotees are pure,
    His kindness marks them safe.
                    Bhairau M1 A1, p. 1153

(4.5)

In ego they come, in ego they go,
In ego they're born, in ego they're dead.
In ego they've given, in ego they're taken,
In ego they've gained, in ego they've lost.
In ego they're truthful and they are liars,
In ego reflecting on virtue or sin,
In ego in heaven or hell they appear.
In ego they laugh, in ego they weep,
In ego they're soiled, in ego they're cleansed,
In ego they lose their status and caste,
In ego they're fools, in ego they're smart,
Not knowing real salvation's worth.
In ego the world, in ego its spell,
By practice of ego, creatures are made.
The gate is opened, grasping ego,[3]
Without wisdom, all is idle talk.
O Nanak, His order sets our fate:
As we see others, we are seen.[4]

Asa ki Var, M1 7.1, p. 466

(4.6)

The nature of ego is this: that in it our actions are done,
The bondage of ego is this: that again and again we are born.
From where does ego arise, what is it that makes it depart?
The order of ego is this: that past actions decide where we roam.
Though ego's an illness that's chronic, it also contains its own cure.
Says Nanak: O hear, everyone, if the Lord only grants us His grace,
To practise the Word of the guru will make all our suffering cease.

Asa ki Var, M2 7.2, p. 466

(4.7)

Whence does it[5] enter birth and death?
Where is it born, where does it merge?
How is it bound, how is it freed?
How does it blend into the Lord?

R. When the Name is in the heart, its nectar on the lips,
Its divine effect grants freedom from desire.

It comes and goes quite naturally,
It's born and merges with the mind.
The guru brings release from bonds,
Through contemplation of the Word.

Birds fly back to the trees at night,[6]
Here we are glad, sad, or astray.
At dawn they look up to the sky,
We wander as our fate decrees.

The Name shows us this world's a hut,
It bursts the jar of lust and rage.
Without the Name, the store is bare
And barred until the guru comes.

He comes as previous fate decides,
Some freely trust him with their lives
And so rejoice in God, the Truth.
I fall, O Nanak, at their feet.

Gauri M1 6, p. 152

(4.8)

Those who take on the mind are the greatest of heroes,
Through their knowledge of self they stay merged in the Lord.
The great mark of the wise is containment in mind,
Fixed on Truth, they discover the house of the Lord.
Through the guru they conquer the mind, so conquer the world.

Maru ki Var, M3 8, p. 1089

(4.9)

Some fools go to the desert
To still the mind, but can't.
O Nanak, it is stilled
Through dwelling on the Word.
It can't be stilled by force,
However hard they try.

The mind will still the mind,
O Nanak, once the guru comes.

Maru ki Var, M3 10.2, p. 1089

(4.10)

When I act in ego, You're not there,
Where You are, no ego can be present.
Understand, O wise ones, understand:
The Word unsaid is present in the mind.
Without the guru, who can find the Real
Which pervades all but cannot be seen?
Once we meet the guru, then we know,
When the Word comes in the mind.
The loss of self removes all doubts and fears,
Along with all the pain of birth and death.
The guru's teaching shows us the Unseen,
And with exalted mind we are delivered.
O Nanak, chant the words 'He's me, I'm Him'[7]
The One in whom the threefold worlds are merged.

Maru ki Var, M1 19.1, p. 1092

(4.11)

Our mind is like a bird
Which bears the deeds we've done
And flies now high, now low.
Now on the sandal-tree
It sits, now on the akk,[8]
Now soars up high in love.
His order drives us all,
For such has always been,
The way, O Nanak, of the Lord.

Majh ki Var, M1 21.2, p. 147

(4.12)

Ego is given man as his disease,
The rutting elephant is sick with lust,

The illness in its vision burns the moth,
Its fevered sense of sound destroys the deer.[9]

R.   Disease afflicts all creatures that appear,
       Except my guru, who remains detached.

Through its disease of taste the fish is caught,
Through its disease of scent, the bee is killed.
The illness of attachment to the world
Of threefold modes causes many wrongs.

Man dies in sickness, in it he is born,
In sickness he keeps wandering through births.
Thus captive to disease he finds no rest,
Without the guru sickness never stops.

To some the Lord Supreme is merciful,
They're led away from sickness by the arm.
The company of saints destroys its grip,
Nanak, the guru has removed disease.

Bhairau M5 20, p. 1140

(4.13)

Attachment,[10] mightiest of heroes,
Whose power breaks the strongest men!
How you beguile all gods and men,
All demigods, all birds and beasts.
    Salute the One who made the world,
    Seek refuge, Nanak, with the Lord.

Lust, you deliver man to hell,
And make him roam through many births!
O stealer of thoughts, found in all worlds,
Destroyer of pious observance!
The pleasure that you give is brief,
You take away all wealth and peace.
    The company of saints removes
    Your fear, O Nanak, through the Lord.

Anger, the basis of all strife,
In whom there is no tenderness!

All sinful creatures in your power
Must act like monkeys made to dance.
Your company makes man debased
And subject to death's punishments.
    O You who save the weak from pain,
    Nanak, from anger save us all!

Greed, close companion of the great,
Your surges make so many twitch!
You make them race and run about,
And lurch and roll unsteadily.
You are without respect for friend,
For guru, parents or for kin.
You're known as one who makes man do
And eat and make what he should not.
    O save me, save me, Nanak says,
    I look to Your protection, Lord.

Ego, the root of birth and death,
You are the very soul of sin!
Betraying friends, you give foes strength,
As you extend illusion's net.
You weary man with birth and death
With knowing many joys and pains.
With roaming in doubt's wilderness
With facing mortal illnesses.
    The only doctor is the Lord,
    O Nanak, we repeat His Name.
        Shalok Sahaskriti M5 45–9, p. 1358

5

SIDDH GOSHT

The *Siddh Gosht* is the title of one of the longest compositions attributed to Guru Nanak in the Adi Granth, where it is printed on pp. 938–46, in the same raga Ramkali as the *Anand* by Guru Amar Das. The content and arrangement of the *Siddh Gosht* are unusual, since it is cast as a debate (Sanskrit *goshti*) between Guru Nanak and the yogic adepts called Siddhs. As is shown by the frequency of references to them, both in the scriptures and in the post-scriptural narratives of the *janamsakhis* and other Sikh writings, the yogic orders, particularly those of the Nath Yogis who derived their authority from the great master Gorakhnath, were a force of major significance in sixteenth-century Panjab. In the *janamsakhis*, Guru Nanak is depicted as successfully engaging in several debates with different groups of yogis, and in the apocryphal literature attributed to him but excluded from the scriptures there are several compositions with yogic themes. The *Siddh Gosht* follows this pattern by using the dialogue with the Siddhs, and the discussion of key concepts like the void (*sunn*) and the Word (*shabad*), to establish the superiority of the Guru's teachings as the true path of yoga.

In keeping with its subject, the *Siddh Gosht* is written in the Sanskritized Hindi used as a lingua franca by the holy men of northern India which is sometimes called Sadhu bhasha. There are many echoes of the crabbed style characteristic of Nath Yogis' own compositions in its 73 stanzas, whose variation in length and internal structure seems to be more casual than the highly patterned formal variations which are so characteristic of the *Japji*. The translation tries to reflect the general predominance here of exposition, often in the half-riddling form favoured by the yogis, over the poetic styles which predominate in most of Guru Nanak's works.

While it is generally clear who is speaking, the Gurmukhi text does not indicate this typographically. Stanzas are often divided between Guru Nanak and his interlocutors, and the transition from one to the other is frequently abrupt. In order to make the structure of the dialogue clear, those verses in which the Siddhs speak are accordingly printed here indented and in italics.

The contents of the main sections of the *Siddh Gosht* may be summarized as follows:

1–3. Introduction to the meeting.
4–6. The Guru answers the opening questions from the yogi Charpat.
7–11. In response to challenge from the yogi Loharipa, the true yoga is explained.
12–22. A series of testing questions, both personal and doctrinal, are posed by the yogis and answered by the Guru.

23–4. The Guru begins a long monologue by describing the origin of creation in the void.
25–6. The fate of the ego-centred and those aware of the Name is contrasted.
27–31. The qualities of the truly guided gurmukh are described.
32–3. Praise of those who are steeped in the Name.
34–5. How the Name is given by the guru to the gurmukh.
36–7. Further description of the gurmukh.
38–9. The necessity of the guru for the attainment of release.
40–2. Further praise of the gurmukh.

43–8. The yogis use the language of yoga to pose a series of riddling questions, which are answered by the Guru.
49–51. The Guru explains the relationship between Word, Name and void.
52–4. Question and answer on the Word and the void.
55–7. Question and answer on right and wrong thinking.

There is only the One, obtained by the grace of the true guru

1

Behold the gathered Siddhs in yogic postures, all hail to the saints'
    assembly!
Since the True and Boundless Lord is here, to it we offer humble
    greeting,
I lay my severed head before it, and offer all my being.
Truth's found through meeting saints, so naturally I'm honoured.

R.   Why wander when the Truth is found through being pure?
      Without the Word that's True, there can be no release.

2

Who are you? What is your name? What is your path? What is your aim?

I speak the truth and only pray to be a sacrifice unto the saints.

Where are you based? Young man, where do you dwell?
Where are you coming from? Where are you going to?
Let Nanak tell us, and hear this too, ascetic: What is your Way?

3

Abiding with the One who pervades all existence, they proceed as
    the true guru pleases,
Entering the world spontaneously and departing by his will, ever
    according to his pleasure.
Sitting unmoving in yogic posture, through the guru's teaching
    they have found the Lord.
The gurmukh understands and realizes himself, and merges with
    the True One.

4

The world is called a sea that's hard to cross, how can it be traversed?
Give us your true thoughts on this, said the yogi Charpat.

To questioners who know the answer how can one respond?
How indeed can I fault you, who've passed beyond the world?

5

Just as a lotus or a duck within the water stays untouched,
So can the world-sea be traversed, through focus on the Word, by
  uttering the Name.
Nanak is a slave to those whose minds remain completely fixed on
  Him alone, desireless in desires,
To those who see and make others see the unperceivable,
  unfathomable One.

6

Listen, sir, to my request, I ask for your true thoughts,
Don't take offence, but tell me how the guru's door is found.

This restless mind sits in its home, when the Name is its support.
The Creator freely unites to Himself, once love is formed for the
  truth.

7

By shops, on roads, by trees, in forests, we remain detached.
To live on roots for food is taught by yogic wisdom,
To bathe at holy sites brings peace of mind and banishes impurity.
This is for sure the way of yoga, said Loharipa, Gorakh's son.

8

By shops, on roads, don't fall asleep, don't let the mind stray off
  abroad
Without the Name the mind is not stilled, its hunger cannot be
  removed
True trade is easy once the guru's shown the shop and town and
  house
Let sleep be broken and food be sparing, Nanak, that is how to find
  the Real.

9

Adopt our yogic teachings and our signs – earrings, wallet and patched coat,[1]
Among the Twelve Orders[2] *and the Six Schools*[3] *follow this one,*
Discipline your mind like this, sir, and so avoid repeated suffering.

Nanak says: understanding through the guru is the key to real yoga.

10

To hold the Word within should be the earrings which keep the self at bay.

Restraining anger, lust and pride through the guru's Word brings understanding.

To sense His presence everywhere should be the coat and wallet of him who is delivered by the Only Lord.

True is the Lord, true is his Glory, who tests for the Word of the guru.[4]

11

Make detachment your begging bowl, the five elements[5] your cap.
Let the body be your mat of grass, the mind your loincloth.
Moderation, contentment and discipline are one's companions,
Nanak, when through the guru the Name is recollected.

12

Who is it that is hidden? Who is it that is freed?
Who is it that is united both inside and out?
Who is it that comes? Who is it that goes?
Who is it that pervades this threefold creation?

13

God is hidden in all hearts, through the guru man is freed,
Through the Word united both inside and out.
The ego-centred perish as they come and go,
Nanak, the gurmukh merges with the True One.

14

How is one chained and consumed by the serpent?
How has one lost? How has one gained?
How is one pure? How is one's sight darkened?
Anyone who can explain this is our guru.

15

Chained by wrong thinking they are consumed by the serpent.[6]
The ego-centred have lost, the gurmukh has gained.
When the true guru comes, darkness departs.
Nanak, destroying the ego allows us to merge.[7]

16

If the mind is bound to the total void,
The wild goose does not fly, the wall does not fall.
Whoever knows that the cave of freedom is his home,[8]
Nanak, is true and pleases the True One.

17

Why have you left your home to become an ascetic?
Why have you adopted this appearance?
What is the stock in which you trade?
How will you lead your followers across?

18

I have become an ascetic to seek for the gurmukhs,
To behold them have I adopted this appearance.
Truth is the stock in which I trade.
Nanak, the gurmukh gets safely across.

19

Young man, how have you transformed your life?
To what have you attached your mind?

How have you consumed your wishes and desires?
How have you discovered the unbroken light within?
How can you eat iron with no teeth?[9]
Nanak, explain this honestly.

20

Those reborn with the guru have ended their roaming,
Those absorbed in the Unstruck have fixed their minds
To the Word which consumes all wishes and desires.
Through the guru the unbroken light within is found
Effacing the three modes[10] lets us eat steel.
This, Nanak, is the way that the Deliverer sets free.

21

What have you to say about the beginning?
Where was the abode of the void then?
What have you to say about the earrings of wisdom?
Who is it that dwells in every living heart?
How can death's cudgel be consumed?
To know the posture of freedom and contentment,
How can one attain the state of fearlessness?

When the guru's Word destroys ego's poison
One dwells in one's true home
Nanak is a slave to those who through the Word
Realize Him who has fashioned creation.

22

Where does self come from? Where does it go?
Where does it stay when merged?
The master who can tell has not a grain of greed.
How can that all-pervading reality be found?
How can it be loved through the guru?
He is both Hearer and Creator.
Nanak, tell us your thoughts on this.

Self comes and goes by nature's order,
By this same order it remains when merged.
Those who through the perfect guru practise truth
Find His state and measure through the Word.

23

As for the beginning, one can only speak in terms of wonder,
For the Lord was then absorbed in void.
Think of the earrings as the uncontrived wisdom of the guru,
Know that the True One dwells in the heart of every creature.
Merger with the Imperceptible comes about through the words of
    the guru,
Spontaneously the state of complete freedom is attained.
With no need for other action, Nanak, through service the disciple
    can find Him.
The order is a mystery, but those whom it makes aware
Know truly the way which creatures should follow.
The real yogi destroys the self, becoming free
Of the world and enshrining truth within.

24

First the imperceptible pure form arises,
Then from being without qualities comes being with all qualities.
Awareness bestowed by the true guru leads to the highest state
Merger with the True is attained through the Word.
Recognizing the One truly as One,
Removing the sense of ego as other,
The yogi understands the guru's Word
Letting his lotus-mind bloom within.
Dying in life, all becomes clear,
As the source of all compassion is discovered within.
Nanak, honour is awarded to those
Who realize the self is connected to all beings.

25

Born from Truth and merging with Truth
The true are pure and are one with the Truth.
The false come but find no place of rest,
In separateness they come and go.
This ceaseless wandering is ended by the guru's Word,
As God both tests and pardons.
Duality brings pervasive suffering
While the elixir of the Name is forgotten.
He understands who is made aware,
Liberated through the guru's Word.
Nanak, the Deliverer saves those who rid themselves
Of ego-sense and duality.

26

The ego-centred wander in the fear of death,
Coveting others' homes they lose everything.
The ego-centred roam deluded in the wilderness,
Lost like evil wizards in cremation grounds,
Unaware of the Word, uttering evil talk.
Know, Nanak, peace comes to all steeped in the Truth.

27

The gurmukh possesses an awe of the True,
The gurmukh uses the Word to order the unordered,
The gurmukh sings praise of the Lord who is pure,
The gurmukh finds the holy and highest state,
The gurmukh reflects on God with total being,
Nanak, the gurmukh merges with Truth.

28

Fulfilled by inner experience,
The gurmukh reflects constantly on the path of wisdom,
Safely crossing the torrent of existence.
The gurmukh through inner experience

Fathoms and discerns the mysteries of the Word.
Attaining the invisible and infinite One,
Nanak, the gurmukh reaches the gate of release.

29

The gurmukh speaks and thinks the unsayable,
The gurmukh is saved while having a family.
Through the guru comes inner invocation with love,
Through the guru God is found in the Word and good conduct,
Pierced by the Word, the gurmukh knows and makes others aware.
Nanak, by burning the ego they merge with their source.

30

For the gurmukh the True One created the world
Where creation and destruction incessantly play.
Dyed in delight with the word of the guru,
They reach their home with honour, steeped in the truth.
Without the true Word no honour is found,
Nanak, without the Name there's no merging with Truth.

31

The gurmukh possesses the eight powers[11] and all understanding,
The gurmukh is aware of the Truth and the world-sea is crossed.
The gurmukh knows the state of good and of evil,[12]
The gurmukh understands worldly life and detachment.
The gurmukh saves and delivers across,
Nanak, the gurmukh delivers through the Word.

32

Those steeped in the Name are free of ego-sense,
Those steeped in the Name are merged with Truth.
Those steeped in the Name realize the way of the yoga,
Those steeped in the Name find the gate of salvation.
Those steeped in the Name are aware of the three worlds,
Nanak, those steeped in the Name are always at peace.

33

Those steeped in the Name get to speak with the Siddhs,[13]
Those steeped in the Name practise permanent discipline,
Those steeped in the Name live in truth and excellence,
Those steeped in the Name understand nature and wisdom,
Without the Name all that is uttered is useless.
Nanak, to those steeped in the Name all hail!

34

The Name is found through the perfect guru,
Remaining merged in Truth is the real way of yoga.
The yogis in their twelve sects[14] wander, the sannyasis in their ten,
Only those who through the guru's Word die in life and attain
    salvation's gate.
Without the Name all are stuck in the sense of duality, realize this
    in your mind.
Nanak, how great and fortunate are those who keep Truth in their
    hearts.

35

The gurmukh finds the jewel through devoted contemplation,
The gurmukh appraises the jewel without effort,
The gurmukh practises actions which are true,
The gurmukh's mind trusts in the True One.
The gurmukh who's favoured is shown the invisible,
Nanak, the gurmukh does not have to suffer.

36

The gurmukh practises the Name, giving and bathing,[15]
The gurmukh is effortlessly absorbed in meditation,
The gurmukh is granted honour in the court,
The gurmukh regards the Breaker of fear as supreme.
The gurmukh performs the actions required,
Nanak, the gurmukh brings others to union.

37

The gurmukh knows Shastras and Smritis and Vedas,
The gurmukh finds the secrets of all in the heart.
The gurmukh gets rid of hostility and conflict,
The gurmukh does away with all calculative thinking.
The gurmukh is steeped in the dye of the divine Name
Nanak, the gurmukh recognizes the Partner.

38

Without the guru, man wanders in coming and going,
Without the guru, all deeds remain fruitless,
Without the guru, the mind is completely at sea,
Without the guru, there is no satisfaction in taking poison.[16]
Without the guru, the snake bites and man dies on the way,
Without the guru, O Nanak, there is loss upon loss.

39

The guru ferries those he meets across,
Removing their vices and redeeming by virtue.
Reflection on the guru's Word brings the great bliss of freedom.
The gurmukh never loses in the game of life.
With the body as shop as the mind as trader,
Nanak, he trades without effort in Truth.

40

The gurmukh is the bridge[17] built by the Creator.
Attacking Lanka, he brings grief to the demons.
Ramachandra destroyed the pride of Ravan,
Through Vibhishan's secret, the guru's instruction.
Through the guru the stones in the sea are delivered,
Through the guru the thirty-three crores[18] are saved.

41

The gurmukh's coming and going is ended,
The gurmukh is granted honour at the court,

The gurmukh discerns the true from the false,
The gurmukh is effortlessly absorbed in meditation,
The gurmukh is absorbed in praise at the court,
Nanak, the gurmukh suffers no constraint.

42

The gurmukh discovers the Name of the Unstained,
The gurmukh burns the ego-sense through the Word,
The gurmukh sings the praises of the True,
The gurmukh remains merged in the True.
The gurmukh gains great honour through the true Name,
Nanak, the gurmukh is aware of all creation.

43

What is the origin? What teaching is this the time for?
Who is your guru? Whose disciple are you?
Whose description keeps you detached?
Let Nanak speak, and explain to us
The One who delivers across the world-sea through the Word.

44

The origin is breath, and this is the time for the guru's teaching,
The Word is my guru, my mind attuned to it is his disciple.
I stay detached through the unspoken Word,
Nanak, of the guru, the Lord through the ages.
Only through the Word can this description be imagined,
The gurmukh quenches the fire of the ego-sense.

45

How can iron be eaten with teeth of wax?
What is the food which makes pride disappear,
Which acts as a garment of fire in a house of snow?
What is the cave which ensures stability?
Who is to be known everywhere and be merged with?
Whom should one deem to be all-pervasive?
By what kind of thinking can the mind merge into itself?

46

Removing the sense of 'I am, and it's me'
Banishes duality and leaves only One.
The world is hard for the fool who is centred in ego,
But through working the Word iron can be eaten,
If the true guru wills, the fire[19] is put out,
Nanak, through knowing the One is within and without.

47

Immersion in fear of the True One banishes pride.
The One is known through reflection on the Word.
When the Word dwells there, Truth is within the heart.
When steeped in the dye, body and mind are cooled.
Lust, anger, poison and the fire are banished,
Nanak, through the glance of the One who is loving and kind.

48

How can the moon enter the house of snow and shadow?[20]
How can the sun keep heating it with its blaze?
How can death be stayed from looking eagerly?
What is the awareness which grants the gurmukh honour?
Who is the warrior who destroys death?
Let Nanak tell us his thoughts.

49

Speaking the Word fills the moon with boundless light,
The sun enters the house of the moon and darkness is ended.
The Name's support makes pleasure and pain the same,
For he is the one who effortlessly delivers across.
Guru-given awareness merges the mind with Truth.
Nanak says: This avoids destruction by death.

50

The Name is the highest of all prayers,
Without the Name pain and death cause suffering.

When true Reality is found the mind comes to believe,
Duality goes and it comes to its one home.
The breath speaks and the sky thunders
Nanak, in bliss unmoving merger is maintained.

51

The void is within, the void is without,
Pure emptiness[21] is the basis of the three worlds.
Whoever knows Him in the fourth void[22] is beyond vice and virtue,
Whoever knows the mystery of the void in all beings
Is as the primal being, the immaculate deity.
Whoever is steeped in the immaculate Name,
Nanak, is as the creator being.

52

Everyone talks of the absolute void
Where does the unstruck void come from?
What are they like, those steeped in the unstruck void?

They are like the One from which they originated,
They are not born, nor do they die, or come and go.
Nanak, through the guru they instruct the mind.

53

When the nine lakes overflow they spill into the tenth,[23]
They sound the trumpets of the unstruck void.
Merged in the True they behold present before them
The True which pervades every being.
The Word's hidden meaning is revealed,
Nanak, to those who distinguish the True.

54

In that state of bliss, union brings joy,
The gurmukh stays awake without sleeping,
Fixing the Word of the void in the divine that is separate.

Freed through reciting it, they save through the Word,
They are steeped in the True through the teaching of the guru.
Nanak, loss of self brings union with no further wandering.

55

Where can it be that wrong thinking is removed?
How is it that non-awareness of reality causes suffering,
That none can protect those tied to death's door,
That without the Word there can be no honour?
How can awareness which leads to deliverance,
Nanak, be roused in the fools who are centred in ego?

56

Wrong thinking is removed by reflecting on the guru's Word.
Meeting the true guru is the gate of salvation.
Unaware of reality, the ego-centred are consumed
By separation and by suffering through false thinking.
Obeying the command[24] brings all virtues and wisdom,
Nanak, it bestows honour in the court.

57

The trader who has truth as stock and coin
Is saved and can save others too,
Steeped in freedom, aware and honoured,
With a value none can realize.
Wherever we look the One pervades all,
Nanak, the love of the Truth brings us across.

58

Where can that Word be said to dwell through which the world-sea may be
     crossed?
The breath is said to span ten fingers' breadth,[25] say, who is its support?
How can the mind which speaks and plays be stilled and let the imperceptible
     be seen?
Listen, swami, let Nanak reach into his mind and tell us this.

The gurmukh who lovingly adores the Word is given favour and
    granted union,
Through great good fortune merging with the One who is all-
    knowing and all-seeing.

59

The dwelling of the Word is ever within,
Present though unseen wherever I look.
As the air is present yet void of presence,
So is it present through an art that's uncontrived.
When through favour the Word enters the heart,
All inner uncertainty is dispelled.
The body, mind and speech are purified,
When the Name is settled in the mind.
Through the Word of the guru the world-sea is crossed
In the knowledge that the One is everywhere
Nanak, recognition of the Word obliterates
Form, colour and the shadow of illusion.

60

The breath that spans ten fingers is sustained,
O yogi, by the non-existent Truth.
When the guru guides speech and reality is distilled,
The Infinite and Imperceptible is known
When the three modes are effaced and the Word is appropriated,
Pride in the ego is removed from the mind.
When inside and outside only the One is known,
Love for the divine Name is experienced.
The awareness that comes from the three yogic channels
Is found through the Imperceptible's free self-revelation.
Nanak, beyond those three lies the True One
With whom the guru's Word brings about merger.

61

Breath is said to be the life-force of the mind
From where does breath draw sustenance?
What is the exercise for attaining knowledge?
What does the adept yogi gain?

Without the Word, nothing can be sustained,
The ego's craving never goes.
Those steeped in the Word who've found the nectar
Are fully sated in the Truth.

What is the knowledge by which the mind stays stilled?
With what food can it be satisfied?

When pain and joy are realized to be the same,
Nanak, the grip of death is broken through the guru.

62

They are not steeped in love, nor drunk in delight,
They are on fire and consumed without the Word of the guru.
Not retaining their seed,[26] not repeating the Word,
Not controlling the breath, not adoring the True.
Describing the indescribable, and making opposites the same,
Nanak, leads to discovering the divine within.

63

Through the grace of the guru they are steeped in the colour of
    love,
They have drunk the nectar and are intoxicated with the Truth.
Meditation on the guru quenches their fire,
Drinking the undrinkable brings them inner peace.
Adoring the Truth, through the guru they have a raft to cross over
    on,
Nanak, how rare is the person who understands this.

64

Where can this raging mind be settled?
Where can this breath be made to stay?
Where does the Word abide, O yogi,
Which ends the wandering of the mind?

When favour is shown and the guru unites,
The mind settles down in its home.
Consuming its self-sense, the mind is made pure,
It is checked from its racing and stopped.

How can the ground be recognized? How can the self be known?
How can the sun enter the house of the moon?[27]

Removal of the inner ego-sense through the guru's guidance,
Nanak, permits entry into the state of bliss.

65

This restless mind is settled in the heart,
When the ground is known through the guru.
The breath has its seat in its home in the navel,
But Reality's found by search through the guru.
The Word dwells forever in its home in the heart,
Through it the light of the three worlds is found.
Hunger for the True eats up suffering,
The appetite for the True is satisfied.
The unstruck sound is known through the guru,
But few are those who grasp its meaning.
Nanak says: Those who praise and are steeped in the True
Are dyed with a colour which never departs.

66

When there was no heart or body,
Where used the mind to dwell?
When the navel's lotus gave it no support,
What was the home of the breath?
When there was no form or sign,
Where was adoration fixed upon the Word?

When there was no hut of blood and semen,[28]
When no price or measure could be found,
When colour, shape and form were hidden,
How could the True be known?

Nanak, by the detached who are steeped in the Name
Then as now the True has been known.

67

When there was no heart or body, yogi,
The mind remained detached in the void.
When it was unsupported by the navel's lotus,
The breath dwelt at home, filled with love.
When there was no form or sign or sort,
The excellent Word dwelt with God without kin.
When the earth and the heavens did not exist,
The Formless itself lit the triple creation.
All colour, all shape and all form
Were simply the One, the Word, the wonderful.
Without the True, none can become pure,
Nanak, this is the untellable tale.

68

In what way is the world constructed?
Through what kinds of suffering does it perish?

Our world is constructed on ego, sir,
Forgetting the Name makes it suffer.
The gurmukh is one who reflects on the wisdom of reality
And destroys ego-sense through the Word.
Mind, body and speech are made pure
Through becoming absorbed in the True.
They are detached who remain in the Name,
With the True One fixed in their hearts.
Nanak, without the Name how can yoga unite?[29]
Look and reflect on this in your heart.

69

Rare is the gurmukh who reflects on the true Word,
To the gurmukh the True One is revealed through the Word.
The gurmukh's mind is steeped, but few understand this.
The gurmukh's dwelling is in his own home.
The gurmukh is the yogi who realizes the Way,
The gurmukh, Nanak, knows the One and Only.

70

Without serving the true guru, there is no Yoga,
Without meeting the true guru, there is no liberation,
Without meeting the true guru, the Name is not attained,
Without meeting the true guru, one finds great suffering,
Without meeting the true guru, one dwells in great darkness of
    pride.
Nanak, without the guru, one dies and loses life's merit.

71

The gurmukh stills the ego-sense and disciplines the mind,
The gurmukh places truth in the heart.
The gurmukh conquers death and never loses life's battle,
The gurmukh does not enter the court defeated
Only the guru's teaching leads to the final joining,
Nanak, the gurmukh knows Him through the Word.

72

Yogi, listen to the final summary of my teaching:
Without the Name there can be no yoga.
They alone attain bliss who are steeped in the Name day and night.
It is through the Name that all is revealed,
Through the Name that awareness is gained.
With no Name many dress up in robes,
The True One has willed they are lost.
It is from the true guru that the Name is obtained.
O yogi, it's then that the way of true yoga is found.

Nanak, reflect in your mind and behold:
With no Name there can be no liberation.

73

Lord, You alone know Your state and Your measure, what more can
    anyone say?
You are visible and invisible of Your own accord, the enjoyer of all
    pleasures.
Many sadhus and Siddhs and gurus and followers roam in search
    through Your will,
To be devoted to experiencing You, when they get the Name that
    they ask for.
Through the true guru one realizes how God the eternal stages this
    play.
Nanak, besides the all-pervading One, there can be no other.

6

ETHICAL BEING

Action and Grace

Once the nature of ego and time are understood to be intrinsically linked, a rather more interesting and complex picture of ethical action emerges from the hymns of the Sikh Gurus than the stereotypical opposition between a passive karma and an active notion of divine grace. For as Guru Nanak states in *Japji*, 'Through deeds we've done we get this garment [of human existence], through grace we reach salvation's gate' (1.4). The linked notions of karma and grace accordingly often appear in the same hymn, underscoring the essentially paradoxical unity between them:

> The deeds you do won't help you in the end,
> For you will reap whatever you have sown.
> There is no other who'll protect you then,
> Besides the saving grace shown by the Lord.
> > Ramkali M5, p. 898

In the teachings of the Sikh Gurus, karma is a law inherent in the nature of existence. Existence itself is depicted by the Gurus as an unfolding of the One, a writing (*lekh*) that is held in place by a fabric made of space, time and cause. The metaphor of writing signifies the nature of the divine One as non-static or continually flowing action. Consequently any action committed by an ego or individuated self, which by definition is separated from the One, works against the flow of divine writing, effectively creating eddies that attempt to freeze the flux of existence. By working against the natural flow, every egotistical action leaves traces of its signature (kar, karni) within the temporal fabric. Instead of simply arising and passing out of existence as would be required by a divine command, these karmic traces accumulate and prolong the separation between ego and the One.

The operation of karma can be likened to the law of conservation of energy except that it is not limited to physical nature but includes the non-physical or psychical aspect of sentient beings: thoughts and speech, desires and feelings. Thus 'good' and 'bad' rebirths are not rewards or punishments but are consequences of specific actions. An action is like a seed which must bear fruit either in this life or the next (6.11). What determines the nature of a karmic seed, however, is the nature of a particular action. Moreover, each and every action (even when this action is intentional as in thought, word, desire or feeling) is imprinted into the temporal fabric of the self, that is, its memory. These imprints are confirmed tendencies, which can be regarded as being somewhat like psychic genes. Actions repeated over time turn into tendencies or habits carried by an individual self through this life and into the next (6.7), unless a way is found to secure release from the imprinting process. Indeed, there are certain meritorious actions which, if performed, stop the imprinting process:

> We repeat that same performance
> Prescribed from the beginning.
> But who can estimate the act
> Of surrender to the guru?
>> Asa M1 A17, p. 420

However, self-surrender or letting go of the ego, as the most meritorious of all actions, requires the intervention of a guru, either in person or through his Word (6.6, 6.8). The person who surrenders his or her mind to the guru is called gurmukh, literally one whose being is turned toward the guru and who no longer performs actions from the standpoint of the ego (6.5, 6.6). In contrast to the gurmukh stand the self-centred (manmukh), who continue to act from the standpoint of ego (6.6, 6.9). The actions of a gurmukh arise in spontaneity (sahaj) so that worldly affairs take care of themselves:

> Your affairs will take care of themselves
> For no one else really makes this happen.
> Rare is the person who knows how to act
> For truth, peace and mercy and righteousness.
>
> Asa M1 10, p. 351

The intertwined nature of karma and grace, of the gurmukh and the self-willed, is perhaps best illustrated by references in the Gurus' hymns to transmigration and the cycle of births and deaths (6.7, 6.15). Insofar as both the gurmukh and the self-willed must perform actions in time, the cycle of births and deaths provides a mythical perspective on time and life which gives rise to sympathy and respect for all living beings (6.13, 6.14). That all existing things and beings are subject to birth, death and passage between different forms (6.12), means that everything that is and that happens is absolutely interconnected, and the only proper starting-point for ethical thinking.

The principal themes of the compositions included in this section may be summarized as follows:

6.1 Rejection of guaranteed rewards for external piety.
6.2 Grace necessary for retrieval from the spirals of wrong-doing.
6.3 Pain and pleasure not opposed but equally necessary in life.
6.4 True merit arises from spontaneous actions.
6.5 A gurmukh's acts are performed without self-effort.
6.6 Contrast between the gurmukh and the self-willed.
6.7 The condition of unregenerate beings.
6.8 How the Name is the key to regeneration.
6.9 Like actions, speech also accumulates karmic traces and is subject to judgement.
6.10 How the gift of the Name is fore-written.
6.11 The emptiness of deeds done without remembrance of the Name.

(6.1)

The flower of the night's first watch
    Yields fruit when dawn is near.
All those whose vigil is maintained
    Receive gifts from the Lord.

Gifts are the Lord's to bestow,[1]
    No one can argue with Him.
Some keep awake unrewarded,
    Others are roused to receive.
        Shalok Farid 112–13, p. 1384

(6.2)

Born from wrong and doing wrong,
    Into wrong they fall.
This wrong cannot be washed away,
    However hard they try.
Unless He chooses to forgive them,
    The blows keep raining down.
        Majh ki Var, M1 24.1, p. 149

(6.3)

O Nanak, it's absurd to ask
    For pleasure, not for pain.
Both pain and pleasure are designed
    As clothes for man to wear.
When speech is bound to make you lose,
    It's better to stay dumb.
        Majh ki Var, M1 24.2, p. 149

(6.4)

To pay a fine while held in chains
Is not an act of merit.
O Nanak, all good deeds are done
By acting willingly.
        Suhi ki Var, M2 7.3, p. 787

(6.5)

The gurmukhs lack all trace of doubt,
They're free from inner care.
Their actions are so effortless
That no more need be said.
Those who belong to Him, O Nanak,
Have their words freely heard.

Bilaval ki Var, M3 9.1, p. 853

(6.6)

The gurmukhs profit through their thoughts
    Fixed on the guru's word.
They gain the riches of the Name,
    Whose treasures have no end.
And through the Word they praise the Lord
    Who has no end or edge.
Nanak, the Creator causes all
    And watches everything.

The balance in the gurmukh lets
    His mind reach highest heaven.[2]
There is no hunger there, just sleep,
    And dwelling with the Name.
Nanak, joy and pain are left behind,
    As God in self appears.

All wear the cloak of lust and wrath
    On entering the world.
Some see the light while others die,
    As the command dictates.
There is no end to birth and death,
    Possessed by other love.
They wander firmly bound in chains,
    There's nothing they can do.
The guru comes to those on whom
    God's mercy is bestowed.
They turn away to die in life
    With spontaneity

Nanak, they who are immersed in Him
    Remain merged in the Name.

The self-willed don't have steady minds,
    Although they may seem smart.
All that they do is done in vain,
    And none of it's approved.
The acts of charity they sow⎤
    Are all consigned to death.⎦
Without the guru, death grips them,
    Lost to their other love.
Youth slips away before our eyes,
    Old age arrives, then death.
Attachment to the family
    Is no help in the end.
The guru's service brings true peace,
    The Name dwells in the mind.
Nanak, the guru lets the fortunate
    Become merged in the Name.

With no awareness of the Name
    The self-willed cry in pain.
They don't adore the God in self,[3]
    How else can they find ease?
They don't employ the Word to cleanse
    The ego's dirt within.
Nanak, without the Name they die in filth,
    And waste this precious life.

The self-willed are both deaf and blind,
    Consumed by their desires.
Without awareness of the Word,
    They can't receive its light.
Without faith in the guru's Word
    They do not know themselves.
The guru's Word within the wise
    Fills them with love of God.
I am devoted to the wise,
    Protected by the Lord

They serve God through the guru's grace,
Nanak, I am their slave.

                              Shalok M3 15–21, p. 1414

(6.7)

Where did those parents belong to,
    And where was the place that we came from?
Fashioned from fluid in fire-pot,[4]
    What purpose is it that we're made for?

R.   My Lord, who knows Your qualities?
      I have too many faults to tell.[5]

How many tree-lives we've witnessed,
    And how many beasts we have been,
How many snake-tribes we've entered,
    As how many birds we have flown!

The thief makes his way into stores,
    Then he brings what he's stolen back home,
Looking before and behind him,
    Yet how is he hidden from You?

We've seen the world's pilgrimage places,
    Its markets and all its bazaars.
The trader who weighs with the scales,
    Is the one who resides in the heart.

The amount of our faults far exceeds
    All the waters of oceans and seas,
Have mercy, O Lord, and be kind,
    Save these stones that are sinking so fast.

This poor soul is devoured with a fire,
    It is stabbed with a dagger within.
Nanak says: Knowing the order[6]
    Brings calm and content night and day.

                              Gauri Cheti M1 17, p. 156

(6.8)

Through the guru the Name is discovered,
The nectar which banishes hunger.
Once the Name comes to dwell in the mind,
No traces of longing remain.
The consumption of anything else
Makes the body a prey to disease.
O Nanak, through feasting on praise
Union's freely attained.

> Sarang ki Var, M3 33.1, p. 1250

(6.9)

With lust and rage and pride within,
The self-willed know not how to speak,
With bad things always in their thoughts,
They can't distinguish right from wrong.
When they face judgement in the court,
They stand revealed as criminals.
  The Same One made the universe,
  The Same One contemplates it all.
  O Nanak, who should be addressed?
  The Same One is in everything.

> Sarang ki Var, M3 30.1, p. 1249

(6.10)

Those whose destiny grants them this power
Remember the Lord through the guru.
Those whose minds find a home for the Lord
Are the targets of Nanak's devotion.

> Sarang ki Var, M3 30.2, p. 1249

(6.11)

The yogis do their yoga, gourmets eat their food
Ascetics practise penance, and bathe at holy sites.

R.   Yours is the call that should be heard,
        Should anyone proclaim it, friend.

We reap as we have sown, we eat as we have earned,
No check is made of those who go approved and marked.

We all are classified according to our deeds,
The breath without remembrance is drawn to no avail.

This body is for sale should any wish to buy,
O Nanak, bodies are no good without the Name. *(God)* *Guru*
                                    Suhi M1 7, p. 730

(6.12)

We're born in a vessel[7] and formed in a vessel,
To a vessel betrothed and espoused.
Around that same vessel relations are formed,
From that vessel the line then proceeds.
Suppose that one vessel should die, then another is sought,
On the vessel the structure is laid.
So how can the vessel deserve condemnation,
When it is the birthplace of kings?
    It's from a vessel that vessels are born,
    None's produced from anything else.
    Nanak, the only exception to this
    Is that Being, the One who is True.
    Nanak, what glory is gained at the court
    By the mouths which are filled with His praise!
                        Asa ki Var, M1 19.2, p. 473

(6.13)

        Conceived from flesh as seed,
        Then placed in flesh as womb,
        There given life, the flesh
        Receives its face and frame.
        Once taken out of flesh,
        It sucks on flesh as breast.
        Its mouth and tongue are flesh,

And in the flesh it breathes.
When it becomes full-grown,
It weds and brings flesh home.
From flesh is flesh produced.
From flesh all ties are formed.
　　To grasp the order through the guru
　　Fulfils the purpose of our lives.
　　We cannot gain our own release,
　　O Nanak, talking is no good.
　　　　Malar ki Var, M1 25.1, p. 1289

(6.14)

'It's flesh, it's flesh', the fool proclaims.
He lacks true wisdom, so can't tell
What's vegetable and what is flesh,
And which it is a sin to eat.

In former times, rhinoceros
Was sacrificed to suit the gods,
Now priests are vegetarian,
They can't stand meat, but feed on men.[8]

Deceitfully they make a show,
Quite unaware what wisdom is.
What use is it to tell the blind?
Nanak, they won't see what they're told.
The blind are those whose acts are blind,
For in their hearts their eyes are shut.

Created from their parents' blood,
Yet they abstain from flesh of fish.
When man and woman join at night,
The couple churn together there.

Conceived from flesh and born from flesh,
We all are vessels made of flesh.
Although the priest may be called smart,
He knows not what true wisdom is.

Can flesh outside be bad, O priest,
While what you have at home is good?

All creatures are produced from flesh,
In flesh[9] they take up their abode.
Directed by the blind, they eat
What they should not, not what they can.

Conceived from flesh and born from flesh,
We all are vessels made of flesh.
Although the priest may be called smart,
He knows not what true wisdom is.

Puranas and Koran describe
The use of flesh through every age.
Both sacrifice and weddings were
Occasions where flesh was approved.
From flesh are men and women made,
So too are kings and emperors.

If it should seem they're bound for hell,
Do not accept their offerings.
It's wrong that givers should be sent
To hell, while takers go to heaven.
Priest, you don't see, but still you preach
To others, how very smart you are!

Do you not even know, O priest,
The source from which flesh is produced?
From water grain, cotton, cane,
Indeed the universe, are made.
Since water can declare it is
Quite pure yet variously transformed,
True abstinence requires one to
Give up all these, so Nanak thinks.

                    Malar ki Var, M1 25.2, p. 1289

(6.15)

Now all the birds gather under the tree,
Some making harsh noises, while others are sweet.
At sunrise they fly off, like man after death.

All those who sin are assuredly lost
Azrael[10] takes and torments them until
Death checks their accounts and they're thrust into hell.

No brothers or sisters accompany them there,
As they go, leaving property, riches and youth,
To be crushed in the mill, unaware of His grace.

You happily stole what belonged to another,
But were seen and were heard by the Lord who is with you
You're thrown in the pit for your greed, so what's next?

Again and again they'll be born and they'll die,
To suffer in torment in far distant lands.
Not knowing their Maker, blind miserable fools.

Those who leave their Creator are lost,
Badly placed in the world, whether happy or sad,
They wander self-willed, and are far from all virtues.

It's the Lord who directs the whole of this play,
Where some are delivered and others are drowned.
By the deeds they've performed, they all dance as He makes them.

If the Lord shows His mercy, my thoughts fix on Him.
To stay with the saints means that hell is avoided.
Give Nanak the Name, let him ever sing praise!

Maru M5 Anjulian 2, p. 1019

What makes an ethical act ethical? to "chance" & help others, to "chance" your love, O God

7

ANAND SAHIB

The raga to which this long composition by the third Guru Amar Das is set is Ramkali, and it is printed on pp. 917–22 of the Adi Granth. The post-scriptural honorific *Sahib* which is commonly attached to the title *Anand*, meaning 'bliss', is an indication of the central importance of key parts of it in Sikh ritual. An abbreviated version consisting of stanzas 1–5 and 40 is recited at the end of the daily evening recitations, of congregational services, and in the rituals prescribed for funerals and for weddings. The distinctive Sikh marriage ceremony (*anand karaj*), which was legally recognized in the Anand Marriage Act of 1909, is itself said to have been originated by Guru Amar Das.

Like most of Guru Amar Das's hymns, the *Anand Sahib* is similar in its linguistic mix of Panjabi and Hindi to that most commonly favoured by Guru Nanak. The style, however, is characteristically more discursive, relying for its effect less upon a packed intensity of expression than upon a progressive use of repetition. The hymn is formally organized in 40 stanzas of somewhat varying length, consisting of an average of five rhyming verses, which are themselves sometimes extended in length, and often beginning with a half-verse. The circular internal arrangement of each stanza strongly emphasizes the opening phrases, which are more or less literally repeated in the first two verses, then reiterated again with the usual poetic signature 'Nanak says' in the final verse.

This structure is perfectly suited to the hymn's subject, the description of the bliss (anand) which is experienced by the devotee through the freedom from suffering and anxiety and the merger of the soul with the divine which are both made possible through following the direction of the guru. While describing the internal process of spiritual transformation, the Anand Sahib is also to be understood in the context of Guru Amar Das's strong development and reinforcement of the institution of the Guruship. Although it is not always possible or appropriate to bring this out explicitly in the translation, many passages clearly refer also to the need for the Sikhs to follow their Guru and to participate in the rituals organized around the singing of the Guru's hymns.

The content of the stanzas may be summarized as follows:

1. The bliss which is conferred by the guru.
2–3. Praise of the divine gifts, especially the gift of the Name.
4–6. The wonderful power of the Name.
7–9. The bliss which comes through the guru.
10–11. The mind is instructed to detach from the world.
12–13. The impossibility of realizing the divine, except through the guru.
14–17. Praise of the saints who are guided.
18–20. Contrast between outward observance and inner devotion.
21–2. The need for the disciple to follow the guru if release is to be gained.
23–5. Invitation to sing the guru's hymns as expressions of the Word.
26–7. How the Creator oversees the world, where some are granted awareness.
28–9. How the divine must be adored through detachment from the world.
30–1. The preciousness of the divine and of repeating the Name.
32–3. Appeal to the tongue and to the body to acknowledge the divine.
34. The mind rejoices in the bliss of experiencing the Name.
35–7. The body, the eyes and the ears are reminded of their real purpose.

38. How the Tenth Door is opened for some, revealing the riches of the Name.

39–40. Invitation to sing in rejoicing at the hearing of the guru's Word.

1

O mother, what bliss I can feel, I have found my true guru.
Without effort[1] I've found him, my mind rings with songs of
    rejoicing,
With their consorts, rich ragas[2] have come to sing hymns.
Sing a hymn to the Lord who is housed in your hearts.
What bliss I can feel, Nanak says, I have found my true guru.

2

O my mind, stay with God at all times,
At all times, O my mind, stay with God the destroyer of pain.
He will accept you for ever and arrange your affairs,
He has power over all things, how can you forget Him?
O my mind, Nanak says, stay with God at all times.

3

Lord, You are true, and Your house is lacking in nothing,
There is everything there, but it's found by the ones whom You
    give to.
Ever singing Your praises, they carry the Name in their hearts,
Many melodies sound in the heart that is home to the Name.
Lord, You are true, Nanak says, and Your house is lacking in
    nothing.

4

My support is the Name that is true,
My support is the Name that is true, which removes every hunger.
Bringing peace, it has entered my heart and fulfilled my desires.
I offer myself to the guru who has such great virtues.
Listen, O saints, Nanak says, and bear love for the Word.
My support is the Name that is true.

5

Heavenly music resounds in that fortunate house,[3]
It resounds in that fortunate house which is filled with His power.

The five evil passions are mastered, and death with its thorn[4] is
    defeated.
Those whose fate was first marked by Your favour are fixed on
    God's Name.
Joy reigns in the house, Nanak says, which is filled with the music
    that's silent.

6

These bodies are weak in the absence of love that is true.[5]
In the absence of love they are weak, poor things, what can they do?
You who alone are all-powerful, be merciful, Lord.
We have nowhere else but the Word to go for adornment.
In the absence of love, Nanak says, poor things, what can they do?

7

Bliss is what everyone asks for, but bliss is attained through the
    guru,
Lasting bliss is attained through the guru, displaying his kindness,
Through his kindness all sins are removed, and the eye-salve of
    wisdom is gained.
Truth's beauty appears in the speech of those freed from delusion.
True bliss, Nanak says, is the bliss that's attained through the guru.

8

Lord, it is found by the person You give to,
It's found by the person You give to, there's nothing that others can
    do.
Some are lost and distracted, some happily fixed on the Name.
Through the grace of the guru made pure, some delight in Your
    will.
O Beloved, says Nanak, it is found by the person You give to.

9

Dear saints, come and tell of the One who is not to be told of,
Let us describe the Ineffable, how can He be found?

Give up all to the guru, obey the command,
Obey the command of the guru, and sing the true Word.
Hear, you saints, Nanak says, come and tell of the One who is not to
be told of.

10

Restless mind, using cleverness no one's discovered Him,
Cleverness never discovered Him, listen to this, O my mind!
The power of this world's an enchantress which leads us astray,
Its power and its magic were made by the One who created the
spell.
I offer myself to the One who implanted this sweetest
enchantment.
Restless mind, Nanak says, using cleverness no one's discovered
Him.

11

My dear mind, you must always remember the True.
This family cannot go with you in death,
Why fix your attention on what will desert you?
Avoid any action for which in the end you'll be sorry,
Hear the true guru's instruction, which always is with you.
My dear mind, Nanak says, you must always remember the True.

12

You are beyond access and reach, and Your limits cannot be
discovered,
Your limits cannot be discovered, and only You know who You are.
All creatures are part of Your game, and so what can anyone say?
You created the world, and You speak and You watch.
You are beyond access, says Nanak, and Your limits cannot be
discovered.

13

Heroes and sages have searched for the nectar that's found through
the guru,

If the guru is kind, the nectar is found, and the True comes to dwell
    in the heart.
Of the creatures You've made, some are drawn to his feet,
To the guru they love, leaving lust, greed and pride.
For those whom he's pleased with, says Nanak, the nectar is found
    through the guru.

14

The way of the saints[6] is quite special,
The way of the saints is quite special, they tread the most difficult
    path,
Renouncing greed, pride and desire, they speak little,
Their way is more sharp than a sword and more fine than a hair.
Through the guru the self is abandoned, desire becomes centred on
    God,
Throughout all the ages, says Nanak, the way of the saints is quite
    special.

15

Lord, we walk as You guide us, what more can I know of Your
    power?
We walk as You guide us, on the way which You show us.
Those Your mercy attaches the Name to, remember the Lord
Whoever You give your account to, finds joy at the gate of the guru
O true Lord, Nanak says, You guide us along as You please.

16

This song of rejoicing is the Word that delights,
The Word that delights us is always the song which the guru
    proclaims.
It resides in the heart of the ones who were destined.
Some wander and talk much, but talk does not find it,
The Word is the song, Nanak says, which the guru proclaims.

17

Made pure are the ones who reflect upon God,
Reflection on God makes them pure through the guru,
Made pure are their parents and kinsfolk and all who are with
 them,
Both speakers and hearers are pure, like those who believe in their
 hearts.
Made pure, Nanak says, are the ones who reflect upon God through
 the guru.

18

No balance[7] arises from rituals, without it anxiety stays,
No efforts dispel this anxiety, for all the rituals done.
Anxiety makes the mind dirty, how can it be cleansed?
By being attached to the Word, and remaining aware of the Lord.
When the grace of the guru gives balance, says Nanak, anxiety goes.

19

Filthy at heart, there are some who are outwardly pure,
Pure on the outside but filthy within, their existence is gambled
 away.
They are gripped by the fever of craving, and death is forgotten,
Like zombies[8] they are deaf to the Vedas, which say that the Name is
 supreme.
In forsaking the truth for the lie, Nanak says, existence is gambled
 away.

20

Some are pure in their hearts and are outwardly pure,
Without and within they are pure, and they act as the guru directs.
Removed from the whisper of falsehood, their will is absorbed in
 the truth,
Those who turn this existence to profit trade well.
Those whose minds are thus pure, Nanak says, are forever attached
 to the guru.

21

If disciples would come to the guru,
The way they should come is by keeping him close to their hearts.
Adoring the feet of the guru, let their minds be devoted to him,
Leaving self, let them trust in the guru, and recognize nobody else.
Hear, O saints, Nanak says, those disciples may come to the guru.

22

By going away from the guru, release is not to be found,
Nowhere else is it found, go and ask those who know.
No release comes without him from roaming through so many
    births,
It is found at the feet of the guru who utters the Word.
Realize this, Nanak says, without him there is no release.

23

Come, followers dear to the guru, sing the hymn⁹ that is true,
Sing the hymn of the guru, the best of all hymns,
It suffuses the hearts of those looked on with favour,
Drink the nectar of loving remembrance of him.
Sing forever, says Nanak, the hymn that is true.

24

Without the true guru all hymns are quite false,
Hymns are all false without the true guru.
Those who speak them or hear them or write them are false.
With God's Name on their tongue, they don't know what they
    speak,
Though their words flow so freely, their heart's with the world.
Nanak says: Hymns without the true guru are false.

25

The guru's Word is a gem which is studded with diamonds.
The mind which is fixed on the gem is absorbed,
Through finding the Word it bears love for the True,

He's the gem and the diamond whose gift brings awareness.
The Word is a gem, Nanak says, which is studded with diamonds.

26

The Creator commands[10] the spirit and matter He's made.
He commands and He looks, letting few understand through the
    guru,
Breaking bonds they are released, with the Word in their hearts.
It is He who can make man a gurmukh absorbed in devotion,
It is He who creates, Nanak says, it is He who explains His
    command.[11]

27

The Smritis and Shastras discuss good and bad, but know not what
    is real,
They don't know what is real, since they don't have the guru.
Lost in the three modes[12] the whole world slumbers on through the
    night
Through the grace of the guru some wake,
    and with God in their hearts are reciting sweet hymns,
They find what is real, Nanak says, by staying awake, having God
    in their hearts.

28

How can you forget Him, who kept you alive in the womb?
How can you forget the great Giver, who nourished you in the
    womb's fire?
No harm can be suffered by those He allows to adore Him,
The gurmukh should always remember the One who allows this.
He is the great Giver, says Nanak, how can you forget Him?

29

The fire in the womb is like the delights[13] which are out there,
Both fire and delights are produced as the sport of the Maker.
The birth of a child, through His will, gives a family joy,

Then craving replaces devotion, delights assume their control,
Delusion arises and God is forgotten, and now the Other is loved.
Even so, through the grace of the guru, says Nanak, He still can be
  loved.

30

God has no price, and God cannot be valued,
He cannot be valued by any, no matter how hard they may try.
God cannot be valued, though men may scream with frustration
If you find a true guru, surrender your life, and let go of your self,
Then the God you belong to will dwell in your mind.
God has no price, and, O Nanak, how lucky are those who have
  found Him.

31

God is my stock, and my mind is the trader,
God is my stock, my mind is the trader, through the guru I know
  what my stock is.
Repeating His Name, fellow creatures, you will make a regular
  profit,
This is the wealth we are given if He should so will it.
God is my stock, Nanak says, and my mind is the trader.

32

O my tongue, while engrossed in these other delights, you con-
  tinue to thirst,
You'll continue to thirst until God is your flavour.
Once God is your flavour, the taste will remove all your thirst.
God's flavour is found through good actions and meeting the guru.
Other tastes are forgotten, says Nanak, once God comes to dwell in
  the heart.

33

O my body, you entered the world after God had infused you with
  light,

Once you were infused with His light, then you entered the world.
It is God who is mother and father, who makes man and who
  shows him the world.
When the guru allows us to see this, the world seems a show that's
  soon over.
When the ground of creation was laid, Nanak says,
  then you entered the world with His light.

34

My mind is rejoicing, it hears that my Lord has arrived,
Sing glad songs in His praise, dear, my home is His palace.
Sing glad songs in His praise, dear, sorrow and grief won't affect
  you.
How blessed are the days when I fall at His feet and adore Him!
In the Word of the guru I've heard the sound that is silent, and
  tasted the Name.
As He willed it, the Lord has arrived, Nanak says, the One who has
  power over all.

35

What have you done, O my body, since you first came into this
  world?
What have you done since you entered this world?
No place has been made in your heart for the God who first made
  you.
If it is so written, He dwells in the heart through the guru.
This body's approved, Nanak says, if the mind is attached to the
  guru.

36

Look only at God, O my eyes, at the One who filled you with light,
No one else should you look at but God, so behold Him.
When you look at this world, what you see is God's form
Through the guru I grasped this, all I see is Him only.
These eyes were once blind, Nanak says, their light is from meeting
  the guru.

37

O my ears, you were sent for the purpose of hearing the truth,
You were sent and were fixed to the body, so hear the true Word
Which refreshes our being and flavours our tongue.
The True is a wonder, it cannot be seen or be told
Hear the Name, Nanak says, be made pure, this is why you were
    sent.

38

God positioned the soul in the cave,[14] and He set the breath playing,
He set it to play, while revealing nine doors and hiding the tenth.
To some devotees through the guru the Tenth Door is shown.
Countless forms and the Name's nine-fold treasures are discovered
    but God has no end,
God the beloved, says Nanak, positioned the soul in the cave,
    and He set the breath playing.

39

Sing this true song of rejoicing, come sing in the house that is true.
Sing in the house that is true, where the True is forever invoked.
Those who please you invoke Him, made aware by the guru,
They receive who are blessed by the Lord universal, True Lord of us
    all.
Sing this true song of rejoicing, says Nanak, come sing in the house
    that is true.

40

Hear my joy, lucky friends, my desires are fulfilled,
I have found the Supreme, all my sorrows have left me,
I suffer no more since I heard the true Word.
On learning the Word from the guru, the saints are delighted.
Those who hear and who sing are made pure by the guru.
For those at his feet, Nanak says, let the trumpets play music
    unheard.

8

GURU AS WORD

The Location of Authority

As one of the central terms in Sikh doctrine, the term 'guru' takes on theologico-political connotations that go well beyond its meaning and application in Hinduism, where it is limited to a teacher of worldly knowledge or a conveyor of spiritual insights. In Sikhism the term guru automatically incorporates this earlier meaning, referring thereby to the personality of Guru Nanak and his nine successor Gurus. Metaphorically it refers to the same divine light manifested in all ten Gurus, and practically it serves to indicate the authority vested in the name 'Nanak'. Thus the hymns of the different Gurus in the Adi Granth are cited by referring to their respective composers as sequential locations (mahala) for the manifestation of the name 'Nanak'. Just before the death of the tenth Nanak, Guru Gobind Singh, spiritual authority was vested in the Adi Granth (henceforth the Guru Granth Sahib), leading to the doctrine of scripture or Word as Guru (shabad-guru).

The logic of this doctrine notwithstanding, the question arises as to who was Nanak's guru? It is worth looking at several ways in which Nanak himself answers this question of who or what was the source of his authority:

> The Word is my guru, my mind attuned to it is his disciple.
> I stay detached through the Unspoken Word
> Nanak, of the guru, the Lord through the ages.
>
> Siddh Gosht (5.44)

> I report the Word of my Lord as it comes to me.
>
> Tilang M1 5, p. 722

Elsewhere, Nanak says: 'I myself do not know how to speak, For as I am commanded, I narrate.' So, despite speaking much, Nanak claims he cannot speak, thereby indicating that it is the Word that speaks and not Nanak. To be vested with authority, Nanak must divest himself of any claim to authority. His self must be silenced by renouncing its authority over what is spoken. There is an echo here of the much older principle of *anhad shabad*, the 'unspoken Word', the Word that resounds without being spoken. The site where the 'unspoken Word' speaks is the mind. By this the Sikh Gurus do not signify revelation in the sense of a communication from a transcendent Being mediated by a human guru. Rather the mind is the true mint in which the formless divine is configured as Word. Insofar as this precipitation as Word occurs in time, the 'unspoken Word' can also be identified as the true guru (*satguru*) which can be regarded as the traceless presence of the divine.

That the 'unspoken Word' is written and spoken in ordinary human language simply points to a notion of the Word's communication that is not between a 'self' and an 'other', but a paradoxical communication of the mind with itself. To say that the 'Word speaks' is to suggest that the circuit of communication arises and ends within the mind. It is not referenced and therefore not authorized by anyone or anything outside. The mind is the source and the target of the Word. This is clearly evident in the Gurus' invocation of 'Nanak' at the end of each verse and hymn. The guru's Word is therefore an exhortation to the mind to become the receptacle for the Name, the purest of all words. Since ego is absent when the 'Word speaks' as 'unspoken Word', one's mind becomes the site of a communication based on the fusion between subject and object, self and other. No longer the passage of words from subject A to subject B, such communication points to the dissolution of knowledge into non-knowledge.

As the following hymns show, there is a fluent interchange between the terms Word (*shabad*), guru (*guru*) and Name (*nam*), all of which are synonymous with ultimate authority in Sikhism, which is defined as the site where ego is lacking. The central ideas that emerge from these hymns may be summarized as follows:

8.1 False gurus as ultimately subject to the turnings of the divine order.

8.2 The guru's Word as cure for the self's craving.

8.3 Life falls apart by ignoring the guru's instruction.

8.4 Mind needs the guru who gives the Name.

8.5 The Word as underpinning all existence.

8.6 Dying to the Word gives true meaning of life.

8.7 The world and the Word.

8.8 The guru brings the wandering mind to its true home.

8.9 The Word as principle of the aesthetic.

8.10 The guru's Word necessary to end the cycle of birth and death.

8.11 The self-centred are devoid of the Name, which the gurmukhs cultivate by dying to the Word.

8.12 The practice of a true Sikh.

8.13 The divine Name as the only unbreakable sacred symbol.

8.14 The nature of the Word as key to discerning between a false guru and a true guru.

8.15 The guru's Word as intersection between human and divine.

8.16 The ecstasy of tasting the Name.

8.17 The authority of Guru Nanak's word.

(8.1)

Disciples play, their teachers dance,[1]
They shake their feet and turn their heads.
The flying dust falls on their hair,
While people look and laugh, then go.
They keep the beat to earn their bread
And fling themselves upon the ground.
They sing as Sitas and King Rams,
As milkmaids and as Krishnas too.
    The One who fashioned all this world
    Is Fearless, Formless, True in Name.
    His servants serve Him with their deeds,
    Sweet nights are theirs whose hearts love Him.
    The guru's teaching is their thought,
    And through his kindness they are saved.
Mills, presses, wheels to pot or spin,
And desert-twisters without end,
Round tops and flails and churning-sticks,
The birds that whirl without a pause,
And creatures turned upon a spit:
All turnings, Nanak, with no end.
    It's He who binds and makes them turn,
    All dance according to their deeds.
    They dance and laugh, then weep and leave,
    But lack the magic art of flight.
    Their hearts delight to dance and leap,
    But hearts which fear are hearts which love.

                    Asa ki Var, M1 5.2, p. 465

(8.2)

Consumed by thirst, the world's on fire,
    Lamenting as it burns to death.
But if the cooling guru comes,
    It does not burn a second time.
So long as they neglect the Word,
    Without the Name, who's free from fear?

              Vadhans ki Var, M3 6.1, p. 588

(8.3)

R.   O mind, you have not grasped the guru's teaching,
     What use are shaven head and ochre robes?

By choosing lies instead of truth,
    Your precious life has gone for nothing,
By using tricks, you've filled your belly,
    And spent your time in beast-like sleep.

Not knowing how to worship God,
    You've sold out to material things.
Caught up with worldly goods, you fool,
    You've not thought of the precious Name.

Unmindful ever of the Lord,
    Your life has been quite purposeless.
Nanak says: O Lord, recall Your grace,
    Your creatures always wander lost.

Sorath M9 10, p. 633

(8.4)

The fire's not put out by dressing in robes,
    The mind still remains taken up with its cares.
To wreck the snake's hole but allow it to live
    Is like doing good deeds with no guru as guide.
Serve the true guru who gives,
    And the Word will reside in the mind.
The mind and the body are cooled,
    The fire of desire is put out.
The highest of joys is attained
    When the self is removed from within.
Those gurmukhs are truly detached,
    Whose minds become fixed on the Real.
Quite content with the Name of the Lord,
    Their cares are completely removed.
Through the Name, Nanak, we may escape
    From the ego's destructive effect.

Vadhans ki Var, M3 6.2, p. 588

(8.5)

The life within all beings is the Word,
Through which we are united with the Lord.
Blind darkness fills the world without the Word,
It is the Word by which it is lit up.
The pious priests may weary studying,
Their bathings may exhaust the ritualists,
Without the Word none can discover Him,
But all must leave in misery and tears.
It is, O Nanak, through His glance of grace
And through His favour that He may be found.

Sarang ki Var, M3 33.2, p. 1250

(8.6)

To die in the Word makes one known after death,
Through the grace of the guru content with the Name,
Through the Word they are recognized there at God's court.
  When the Word is not there, all are dead anyway,
  The life of those centred on ego is vain,
  Forgetting the Name will bring grief in the end.
Whatever the Maker performs comes to pass

Shalok M3 43, p. 1418

(8.7)

The madness of the world without the Word is not to be described.
All those whom God protects are saved, the Word absorbs their
    love.
The Maker made the world and, Nanak, He knows everything.

Shalok M3 36, p. 1417

(8.8)

Quite lost, I wander round
But none tells me the way.
Please ask the ones who know:
Can someone stop my pain?

The mind that holds the guru
Becomes the dear Lord's home.
Nanak, it is made content
Through praise of the True Name.
> Maru ki Var, M1 3.1, p. 1087

(8.9)

The Word adorns the tongue
Which chants 'How Wonderful!'[2]
The Word most perfect brings
The meeting with the Lord.
How fortunate are they
Who cry 'How Wonderful!'
Folk come to honour those
Made lovely by this chant.
Grace grants 'How Wonderful!'
With honour at the gate.
> Gujri ki Var, M3 14.2, p. 514

(8.10)

With no faith in the guru, with no love for the Word,
Even hundreds of births cannot ever bring peace.
Nanak, the gurmukh is easily joined through his love with the Real.
> Vadhans ki Var, M3 14.1, p. 591

(8.11)

The self-centred lead lives that are cursed,
They never give thought to the Name.
Their minds give no place to the Source
Of the food and the clothes they enjoy.
Can the mind that's not pierced by the Word
Ever hope to discover its home?
Their coming and going destroys
The self-centred, like wives who've been left.
For the gurmukhs, the Name is their bliss,
The jewel that's engraved on their foreheads.

Since the Name of the Lord's in their hearts,
There the Lord is in bloom like a lotus.
Their hearts hold the Name of the Lord,
Their Lord like a lotus in bloom.
The guru's attendants inspire my devotion,
Nanak, how bright are the faces lit up by the Name!

Successful are those who die in the Word,
Without which there is no salvation.
When inspired by the love of anything else,
Robes and rituals lead to destruction.
The guru is needed for finding the Name,
Nanak, no matter how much it is longed for.

God's Name is very great and high,
It's higher yet than high.
However burning their desire,
None can ascend to it.
To roam in robes makes no one pure,
Nor talk of self-control.
To get to climb the guru's stair
Is something gained by grace.[3]
The guru enters into those
Who contemplate the Word.
Death in the Word allays the mind,
Nanak, true fame lies with the True.

                                    Shalok M3 31–3, p. 1416

(8.12)

Let those who'd be called true Sikhs of the Guru[4]
    Rise early and ponder the Name.
Let them busy themselves at the time of the dawn
    And bathe in the pool filled with nectar.[5]
Reciting[6] the Name as the Guru has taught
    Will remove all their sins and transgressions from them.
Let them sing after daybreak the Word of the Guru
    And ponder the Name in all acts they perform.
Those who ponder our Lord with each breath that they take
    Are true Sikhs who make happy the mind of the Guru.

All those who are blessed by the merciful Lord
   Are true Sikhs who receive the Guru's instruction.
Nanak humbly craves dust from the feet of the Sikh
   Who utters the Name and gets others to do so.

                                   Gauri ki Var, M4 11.2, p. 305

(8.13)

The true sacred thread comes from praising the Lord
Its genuineness comes through accepting the Name.
When this sort of thread is worn at the court,
It will never break and is sacred indeed.

                                   Asa ki Var, M1 15.4, p. 471

(8.14)

Meeting the guru brings joy to the mind,
   Like the earth when renewed by the rains,[7]
Everything looks so refreshed and so green,
   As the ponds and the lakes overflow.
The being within is infused with the Truth,
   Like the madder-plant dyeing things red,
The lotus of Truth comes to bloom in the mind,
   Which the Word of the guru makes glad.

Pay careful attention to those led by self,
   Who are going a different route.
Like deer in a trap they are captured by death,
   Which stands hovering over their heads.
Thirst, hunger and blame are all bad
   And anger and lust are repulsive,
But they cannot be properly seen by these eyes,
   Till attention is paid to the Word.

If You so desire, the contented are freed
   Of all everyday cares in this life,
By serving the guru our stock is established,
   For he is our ladder, our boat.
Reality, Nanak, can only be grasped
   When the Truth comes to dwell in the heart.

                                   Malar ki Var, M3 1.1, p. 1278

(8.15)

Do not forget the Name,
Recall it day and night.
Your mercy keeps me safe,
From that comes all my joy.

R.   I am blind and the Name of the Lord is my stick
     If I trust in the Lord, I am freed from delusion.

Wherever I should look,
The guru shows You're near.
I search inside and out,
And find You through the Word.

The guru lets me love
Your Name, O Stainless Lord.
Dispeller of all doubts,
I'm guided by Your will.

The fear of death afflicts
Us all from when we're born.
But birth and death are blessed
Through singing praise to God.

I am nothing, You exist
And You have made all this.
You make and You destroy,
You favour with the Word.

The body turns to dust,
Where does the soul go then?
The wonder is that You
Are found in everything.

You're never far, O Lord,
We know that all is You.
The guru lets us see
You're out there and inside.

Let me dwell in the Name
And know true inner peace.

The guru's teaching, Nanak,
Moves devotees to praise!
                    Suhi M1 A5, p. 752

(8.16)

No other taste of all you've tried
Can grant you slight release from thirst.
But of the Name a single taste
Will make you drunk with ecstasy.

R.   Drink the nectar, my dear tongue,
     Drink your fill of its delights!

Sing praises of the Lord, my tongue,
In every moment ponder Him.
The company of saints is gained
By luck, so hear and stay with them.

Adore Him night and day, my tongue,
The Lord supreme and fathomless.
Made precious as you praise the Name,
Be ever happy in both worlds.

Though flowers may yield the sweetest fruits,
This taste once known cannot be left.
The Name surpasses all delights,
Nanak, for those the guru aids.
                    Gauri Guareri M5 15, p. 180

(8.17)

While mercy goes on being freely given,
There never can be any want or shortage.
So too the use and spending of its treasure
Cannot exhaust the Word of Baba Nanak.
                    Shalok M5 20, p. 1426

9

SHABAD HAZARE (PATSHAHI 10)

While the somewhat mysterious title *Shabad Hazare* does not itself appear anywhere in the scriptures, it is given to two sets of hymns (*shabad*) which are recited as a part of their daily devotions by the devout. The meaning of the unusual word *hazare* or *hajare* has been variously explained; it is generally understood as deriving from *hazar*, 'thousand', with the presumed idea that the recitation of these 'Hymns in a Thousand' earns the devotee thousand-fold merit.

The first set of *Shabad Hazare* is a group of seven hymns in various ragas from the Adi Granth, one by Guru Arjan and six by Guru Nanak, which are printed together under this title in the standard devotional handbook (*gutka*). The other set, translated here, consists of ten compositions by Guru Gobind Singh, which appear together in the Dasam Granth (pp. 709–12), and are distinguished by the title 'Patshahi 10' or 'Tenth Kingship'.

Nine of these compositions are hymns in different ragas of the general type which is so common in the Adi Granth, but which is otherwise hardly represented in the Dasam Granth. Clearly forming a set, they are all written in the same formal structure, opening with a refrain that starts with a short and striking initial phrase, then containing three verses. As with much of the rest of the Dasam Granth, the style is more formal than most of the hymns of the earlier Gurus. These nine hymns are all written in Braj Bhasha, with the plentiful use of Sanskritic words typical of the Guru's other compositions. The language and style are in keeping with their questioning of traditional Hindu practices and beliefs, whose true meaning is reinterpreted in the light of the Guru's teaching. Hymns 9.1 and 9.2 explain the practice of true yoga, and 9.3 teaches the need to wake up from worldly delusion. In 9.4 numerous epithets of Vishnu are used to praise God, while 9.5 and 9.6 criticize the mythologies associated with the god and his manifestation as Krishna. The indefinable Creator is praised in 9.7, His power is contrasted with the futility of worshipping stone images in 9.8, and His transcendence of all Hindu and Muslim definitions is the theme of the concluding hymn 9.9.

The other composition included as the sixth item of Guru Gobind Singh's *Shabad Hazare* is quite different from the others, and its placement in their midst is one of the many puzzles of the Dasam Granth. In the scriptural context, it is exceptional in being written in Punjabi and being composed very much in the popular style of a folksong in which a girl cries out from the luxury of her surroundings for her absent lover, and both these features help to account for its exceptional popularity. Since it is so unlike the rest of the *Shabad Hazare* in style and content, it is translated separately here:

> Tell the Friend whom we all love
>   The state of His disciples:
> Sickened by these quilts without You,
>   Our mansions are like snakes' nests.
> Flasks are torture, cups are knives,
>   We're cut by butchers' choppers.
> Longing for His simple bed,
>   We curse this rich existence.
>
> Khyal Patshahi 10, 6

(9.1)

R. O mind, let this be your detachment:
  Your home is quite sufficient jungle
  To be a hermit in the heart.

With effort as your locks, with yoga as ablution
  Grow the nails of observance.
With wisdom as your guide, afford your soul instruction
  Make the Name your body's ashes.

With very sparing diet, sleeping very little,
  Cherish mercy and forgiveness.
By all the time adopting patience and forbearance
  Pass beyond the threefold modes.

The mind should be kept free from lust, pride, greed and anger,
  From perverse infatuation.
This way alone gets us to see the self's true nature
  And to grasp the Highest Being.
                                    Ramkali Patshahi 10, 1

(9.2)

R. O mind, make this your yogic practice:
    Make truth your horn, sincerity your necklace,
    Smear on remembrance as your ashes.

Make heart's restraint your instrument
    To beg as alms the Name's support.
Pluck the string of God's reality
    To play the tune of ecstasy.

These songs of wisdom will produce
    Delightful waves of melody.
Astounded, demons, gods and sages
    Enjoy them in their heavenly seats.

Instruct your soul garbed in restraint
    And silently recite the Name.
The body thus becomes like gold
    Safe from the ravages of death.
                                    Ramkali Patshahi 10, 2

(9.3)

R. O mortal, grasp the Highest's feet!
    Shaking off delusion's slumber,
    Wake up and stay alert!

Dumb beast who lacks all understanding,
    How can you preach to others?
Why be so fond of evil things?
    Abandon their attractions.

Know that those deeds just lead to error,
    Love righteousness instead.
Remembrance is what you should gather,
    Give up and run from sin.

Thus you'll escape all grief and sin
    And slip the noose of death.
If you desire all happiness
    Be steeped in love of God.

Ramkali Patshahi 10, 3

(9.4)

R. What honour, Lord, have I but you?
    Blue-throated, lion-man, Narayan,
    Blue-clad, and flower-garlanded.

Supreme being, highest lord,
    Pure one, who lives on air.
Madhav, mighty light, Madh-slayer,
    Murar and Mukand.[1]

Unchanging, ageless, never sleeping,
    Sin-free, who wards off hell.
The lord of time, compassion's ocean,
    Who cancels evil deeds.

Bow-bearer, patient, earth's supporter,
    Wielder of the sword.
My feeble mind seeks your protection,
    Hold me, set me free.

Sorath Patshahi 10, 4

(9.5)

R. Believe not in what's made but in the Maker:
    Know He's the Highest, Primal Lord,
    Not born or conquered or destroyed.

So what if in this world once Vishnu
    Slew some ten-odd demons,
And making a great show persuaded
    All to call him Brahma?

Why think him Creator, Breaker
    Powerful, eternal?
For he himself fell victim to
    The sword of death the mighty.

He was drowned, fool, in the world-sea,
    How will he save you then?
Death's escaped by holding him who
    Was before the world was.

                        Kalian Patshahi 10, 5

(9.6)

R. Time alone is the Maker.
    Beginning and end, of infinite form
    The One who creates and destroys.

Praise and blame are one to Him,
    He has no friend or foe.
What should have led Him to become
    Arjun's charioteer?[2]

Saviour with no family,
    He has no caste or kin.
Why should He be called the child
    Of Nand and Devaki?

He made the gods and demons, these
    Dimensions and expanse.
How can He be truly praised
    By naming him 'Murar'?

                        Tilang Patshahi 10, 7

(9.7)

R. How can He be in human form?
Exhausted in their contemplation
The Siddhs have failed to see Him.

Narad, Vyas, Parasar, Dhruv[3]
Have practised meditation.
Vedas and Puranas strive no more
To think what He is like.

Gods, demons, ghosts and goblins
Say 'it's not this, not that'.[4]
Some have thought Him super-fine,
Some say He's super-great.

He's made heaven, earth and hell
He's called both one and many.
Escape from death's noose comes to those
Who shelter at God's feet.

Bilaval Patshahi 10, 8

(9.8)

R. Distinct as one who has no other,
As Creator, ever-powerful,
Who makes and breaks He's known.

What good is it to worship stones
With love and adoration?
Through rubbing rocks your hands are worn
To no result at all.

You offer rice and lamps and incense
What does that stone consume?
What power does it possess, you fool,
What blessing can it give?

If living, it might benefit
Your mind and words and deeds.
Only refuge with the One
Can grant deliverance.

Devgandhari Patshahi 10, 9

(9.9)

R. Without God's Name none can be saved.
    How can we flee from Him
    Who rules the fourteen worlds?

Ram and Rahim[5] will not save you,
    Though you repeat their names.
For all the gods, and sun and moon
    Are subject to death's power.

The Hindu and the Muslim books
    Say 'it's not this, not that'.
Snake,[6] Indra, and the sages failed
    To think what he is like.

His form and colour are unknown,
    Why should we call Him Dark?[7]
Escape from death's noose can be gained
    By clinging to God's feet.

Devgandhari Patshahi 10, 10

10

COMMUNICATING ECSTASY

Knowledge and Non-Knowledge

Accounts of mystical experience have tended to suggest that silence and ineffability are the best characterizations of the mystical state. It is not surprising therefore that attempts by mystics to communicate this experience, either by speaking or by writing about it, have generally invited suspicion, being regarded as a violation or betrayal of the interiority of mystical experience by exteriorizing it. Yet this is clearly at odds with the fact that the profoundest mystics have shown a deep and abiding will to communicate knowledge of their experience to others. And the Sikh Gurus were certainly no exception.

Apart from Guru Nanak's very clear account in *Japji* of his own spiritual experience as a trans-subjective journey through the various *khands* (1.34–7), Sikh scripture is replete with verses that narrate a certain knowledge about the ecstatic state. What is clear, though, is that this 'knowledge' cannot stem from the standpoint of the isolated or inflated ego that obstructs the path to liberation by standing in opposition to anything that is 'other' (10.9, 10.12). For the Gurus, knowledge that stems from this standpoint is patently false, for it leads ultimately to the hypocrisy of the scholar, the ritualist or the politician (10.1, 10.10, 10.22, 10.23, 10.24), or indeed the adulterous spouse (10.2, 10.3, 10.4, 10.8, 10.11), for whom the experience of the divine is foreclosed. For such people the only experience is experience of the other as object.

For the Gurus, however, true knowledge results only from fusion or merger of self and other, which, while it dissolves the category of 'self' and 'other', nevertheless allows a paradoxical emergence of a consciousness that witnesses and is witnessed by the other (10.13, 10.14, 10.19, 10.20). This is not an experience where the mystic 'decidedly' remains in silent satisfaction of a self-absorbed bliss. Rather, descriptions of the state of fusion reveal a dynamic counterpoint between two opposing desires: the desire to merge into the other, and the simultaneous desire to be differentiated. Far from being annihilated or silenced, the self that emerges from the ecstatic experience, insofar as it can speak of its experience, emerges as singular and plural, a site of absolute interconnected-ness to others. By thus invalidating the supposed opposition between divine transcendence and immanence, the standpoint of the ecstatic is revealed as an entirely worldly experience, and should be regarded as the touchstone of morality and politics.

The following main themes characterize the compositions included in this section:

10.1 The hypocrisy of exterior ritual compared to true wisdom.
10.2 The soul's pain and ecstasy symbolized through the bride's separation from her Beloved.
10.3–5 The ego's isolation depicted as the bride without virtue, while the bride who cultivates virtues pleases her Lover who remains ever close.
10.6 Happiness resides in devotion to one's parental and in-laws' homes.
10.7 The bliss of union likened to the constant presence of the Spouse.
10.8 True bliss comes from faithful devotion to the Name, the true 'object' of love.
10.9 The ecstasy of the soul that yearns for its Beloved to come.
10.10 The futility of finding God through knowledge.
10.11 The bliss of merger is beyond such dualisms as good and bad.
10.12 Relinquishing ego, ecstatic bliss is found in merger.
10.13 Pure witnessing arises with the fusion of self and other.

10.14 Paradoxical descriptions of freedom in fusion, and self-discovery as void of bliss.

10.15 Dying to the self gives rise to wisdom and contentment.

10.16 Killing mind and ego as the touchstone of divine presence.

10.17 True mindfulness is beyond acts of discipline.

10.18 Unity of mind and matter as the underlying truth of existence.

10.19 Non-knowledge of divine immanence arises through dissolution of 'subject' and 'object' of experience.

10.20 To know the divine is to experience non-knowledge.

10.21 Love as a requirement for gaining true wisdom.

10.22 The hypocrisy of today's leaders who pretend to lead on the basis of knowledge.

10.23 Leaders profess wisdom, but true wisdom begins with renunciation of ego.

10.24 Union eludes those who profess to know.

10.25 The merest trace of the Name gives rise to knowledge as non-knowledge.

10.26 No physician can cure the mind's longing for unity.

10.27 Mind's liberation comes through selfless devotion to the Name.

10.28 The rapture of fusion comes from knowing that the self knows nothing.

(10.1)

They read their books,[1] they pray, and they debate,
They worship stones and stand like cranes[2] in trance.
They use fair words to hide the lies they tell,
And regularly pray three times a day.
With garlands and their sacred forehead marks,
They have two loincloths and keep covered heads.
    But all these acts seem futile, once it's known
    What Brahma and what karma really mean.
    Say, Nanak: let them meditate with faith,
    Without the guru none can find the way.

                      Shalok Sahaskriti M1 1, p. 1353

(10.2)

When I look in my heart, my Beloved is with me.
Nanak says: Through His grace all my grief is removed.

Nanak longs to hear of Him
Whose court so many wait upon.
Lord, You know of my desire
Ever to behold Your face.

What's this, you fool, another's wife?
Look rather to the Lord
Though, Nanak, like a bed of flowers
This world is full of blooms.

                    Maru ki Var 2, M5 4.1–3, p. 1095

(10.3)

    The sluttish bride may think she's fair,
        But she is black and foul at heart.
    It's virtues that delight the Lord
        But, Nanak, all she has are faults.

                    Maru ki Var, M1 5.1, p. 1088

(10.4)

The bride who behaves well delights the whole family,
Deriving her goodness from love of her husband.
Maru ki Var, M1 5.2, p. 1088

(10.5)

The husband is pleased with the bride
 Whose heart is adorned with the Name.
O Nanak, what glory belongs
 To her when she stands before Him!
Maru ki Var, M3 6.1, p. 1088

(10.6)

At their parents' and in their new home[3]
 They belong to the Fathomless Lord.
O Nanak, how happy are those who delight
 The One who's beyond all concern.
Maru ki Var, M1 6.2, p. 1088

(10.7)

The Beloved belongs to them all,
 And none are bereft of the Lord.
O Nanak, those brides who are merged
 In the guru know marital bliss.
Maru ki Var, M3 7.1, p. 1088

(10.8)

The wretched bride goes wearing red[4]
To lie with someone else's man.
Her husband's left behind at home,
Another love seduces her.
Though she enjoys its sweet delights,
It only makes her illness worse.
She's left her husband, the True Lord,
And now she suffers in His absence.

She whom the guru turns from this
Has God's love as her ornament.
She loves her One True Lord in bliss,
And holds His Name within her heart,
With her Creator she is merged,
A dutiful and happy bride.
Say, Nanak, how the True Lord's wife
Is always happy with her Mate.

Suhi ki Var M3 1.1, p. 785

(10.9)

I am in love with Him, how can I find my Love?
I search for my dear Love, who is adorned with truth.
The guru is my friend, to whom I'm sacrificed,
Who's shown to me my Love, my God and dear Creator.
I looked elsewhere, the guru showed me He's with me.

I stand and watch the road in case my Love arrives.
I long to be united with my Love today.
I would be sacrificed to one who showed me Him.
The guru meets us if the Lord is merciful.

While ego rules, illusion's cycle is maintained,
The guru's not obeyed, the world-sea is not crossed.
Those favoured by the look[5] walk as the guru wills,
To see the guru grants us all that we desire.
Those who accept the guru find me at their feet,
Attuned to love within, they've Nanak as their slave.

How can those who're in love with the Lord
Be happy unless they can see Him?
Through the guru they easily find Him,
And thus are their minds filled with joy.

How can those who're in love with the Lord
Live without Him whom they hold so dear?
O Nanak, it's when they behold Him
That they are renewed and refreshed.

Through the guru they love You within,
They are drowned in true love day and night.

Through the guru, O Nanak, true love for the True
Immerses in balance and permanent bliss.

Shalok M4 4–10, p. 1421

(10.10)

Read on, read on, fill carts and caravans,
Read on, read on, fill boats and pits,
Read on for all your months and years,
Read on for all your life and breaths.
Nanak, only one thing counts, the rest is rot.

Asa ki Var, M1 9.1, p. 467

(10.11)

To fall for someone else is no true loverhood,
The lover's name belongs to those whom love absorbs.
To take good treatment well and take bad treatment ill
Is just to keep account, and is no lover's part.

Asa ki Var, M2 21.1, p. 474

(10.12)

Kabir says: freedom's gate is tight,
A tenth part of a tiny seed.
This mind is like an elephant,
So how on earth can it get through?
If, though, a guru can be found
Who's pleased and wishes to be kind,
The gate of freedom opens wide,
Allowing easy passage past.

O Nanak, freedom's gate is tight,
The very small alone can pass.
When ego's swollen up the mind,
How can it hope to pass that gate?
It's when the guru comes to us

That ego goes and all is light.
At last this soul finds its release
And always stays absorbed in bliss.
Gujri ki Var, Kabir 4.1, M3 4.2, p. 509

(10.13)

The Same One's school and teacher,
The Same One[6] makes them learnt.
The Same One is the parents
Who educate the child.
The Same One learns it all
Or stays quite ignorant.
The Same One summons some,
Approved as being true.
Blessed through the guru they
Are known at the True Court.

The Same One's sage and singer,
And tells the Six Schools' message.
The Same One's all the gods,
And speaks the Unsaid Word.
The Same One both enjoys
And leaves all things behind.
The Same One teaches wisely
And argues on both sides.
The Same One makes the play
And watches, knowing all.
Bihagre ki Var, M4 11–12, p. 552

(10.14)

It's those whom He desires that are
    Entitled 'servants of the Lord'.
For Nanak knows that He is not
    To be distinguished from His saints.

As water blends with water,
So light should blend with Light.
Thus merged with the Creator,

The self is known within.
The void of bliss is entered,
The One alone is found,
Both immanent and free,
In self-descriptive state.
Doubt, fear and modes depart,
As water blends with water.

Vadhans M5 C2.4, p. 578

(10.15)

The teachings of the wise apply to all the world.
The gurmukh fears the Lord and learns to know the self.
Through dying while alive, the mind grows self-content.
Without trust in the mind, what wisdom can be preached?

Sorath ki Var, M3 12.1, p. 647

(10.16)

Kabir, the false all fail the touchstone of the Lord.
The dead-in-life alone can pass its test.

How can this mind be killed, how can we make it dead?
Unless the Word's believed, the ego can't be left.
The guru's grace stops ego, and makes one dead-in-life.
O Nanak, once it's granted, no obstacles remain.

They talk of 'death-in-life', how can that state be found?
By dieting on fear, with love as medicine.
The Name delivers those who ever sing glad praise.
To those He favours, Nanak, through the guru it will come.

Ramkali ki Var, Kabir 4.1, M3 4.2–3, p. 948

(10.17)

No penance or devotion works,
For all is gained through mindfulness.
The mindful, Nanak, gain regard,
The guru's grace makes them aware.

Ramkali ki Var, M2 14.2, p. 954

(10.18)

The merger of body and spirit
Was written first by the Creator
Who's hidden yet everywhere present,
Revealed and shown forth by the guru.
Through telling and praising His virtues,
Those virtues then come to absorb us.
We are Truth through the Word that is true,
The Truth unites all to itself,
Existent and present in all things,
Bestowing its greatness upon them.

Ramkali ki Var, M3 14, p. 954

(10.19)

It is You who are water, and You are the fish,
   It is You who are also the net.
It is You who's the one that is casting the net
   And You are the slime[7] that's within it.
It is You who're the lotus, untouched and untainted,
   Whose colour remains in the depths.
It's You who secure the release of all those
   Who give You the briefest of thoughts.
There is nothing beyond You, Lord who's beheld
   In delight through the Word of the guru.

Srirag ki Var, M4 7, p. 85

(10.20)

How to die within life:
   See without eyes,
   Hear without ears,
   Walk without feet,
   Work without hands,
   Speak without tongue.
Nanak, know the command
And come to your Lord.

Majh ki Var, M2 3.1, p. 139

(10.21)

Though he be seen and heard and known,
His essence can't be caught.
How can the lame and halt and blind
Run into His embrace?

With feet of fear and hands of love
And eyes which are aware,
Smart girl, says Nanak, that is how
You'll come to find your Love.

Majh ki Var, M2 3.2, p. 139

(10.22)

Though telling lies and using what's not theirs,
They keep instructing others what to do.
Since they're misled, those with them go astray.
Such, Nanak, are the leaders that we find.

Majh ki Var, M1 5.1, p. 140

(10.23)

I am nothing,
What can I say?
I have nothing,
What can I do?

All my actions,
All my words
Are full of sins
For me to cleanse.

I don't know me,
I tell others.
Is this the way
For me to lead?

Nanak, when the blind
Point out the way,
All those with them
Become quite lost.

When they pass on,
Such leaders get
The treatment that
Shows who they are!

Majh ki Var, M1 6.2, p. 140

(10.24)

Union eludes these robes, this theory and technique.
Nanak: gnosis[8] comes through mercy to the devotee.

Gnosis is not gained through words upon the lips,
Or through different methods written in the Shastras.
They are the true gnostics in whom He's firmly fixed.
Union eludes all those who simply talk and listen.
Gnostics have His order firmly fixed,
Pains and pleasures are the same to them.
Nanak, if His mercy's granted them,
Through the guru gnostics know reality.

Gauri Bavan Akhari M5 5, p. 251

(10.25)

We seek sanctuary with You, O Lord most merciful!
Nanak, happy are the minds in which one letter[9] dwells.

Through the letter the Lord has established the threefold creation,
Through the letter the Vedas are fashioned and commented on,
Through the letter come Shastras and Smritis, Puranas,
Through the letter come singing, reciting and teaching,
Through the letter comes freedom from doubt and delusion,
Through the letter come acts which are righteously done,
Through the letter comes all that is seen,
Nanak, except for the Lord who's untouched.

Gauri Bavan Akhari M5 54, p. 261

(10.26)

Our pains are those of separation,
Craving, fearing mighty death,

And illness that attacks the body.
    Unskilled physician, stop your treatment.

R.   Unskilled physician, stop your treatment.
    There's no need for a cure, my friend,
    Which does not take the pain away.

When pleasures mean the Lord's forgotten,
Disease arises in the body,
The foolish mind then suffers.
    Unskilled physician, stop your treatment.

The point of sandal is its scent
The point of man is living breath
When breath departs, the body rots.
    And then who asks for medicine?

That body's gold, that soul is pure,
Which hold a portion of the Name,
To make all illness disappear.
    The True Name, Nanak, grants release.
                     Malar M1 7, p. 1256

(10.27)

Upon the dish[10] three things are placed:
Truth, contentment, and reflection.
On it the Lord's Name too is placed,
The Nectar which sustains us all.
To those who eat it with delight
Release is granted as reward.
This thing cannot be set aside,
Keep it close beside you always.
Cling to His feet and be delivered
Across the dark sea of this world.
Nanak, all stems from the Lord.
                  Mundavani M5, p. 1429

(10.28)

How little I've known all You've done
In making me ready for service.
I am lacking in merit and virtue,
It is You who have shown Your compassion.
You have granted Your grace and Your mercy,
I have met with my friend, the true guru.
Nanak, the Name of the Lord grants me life
And it fills my whole being with rapture.

Shalok M5, p. 1429

11

ZAFARNAMA

Included in the final section of the Dasam Granth (pp. 1389–94), the *Zafarnama* or *Epistle of Victory* is composed in Persian as a heroic poem in the style of Firdausi's classic Persian epic the *Shahnama* or *Book of Kings*. It takes the form of a letter from Guru Gobind Singh to the Mughal emperor Aurangzeb, and presupposes some knowledge of the tragic events of December 1704 which initiated the final phase of the Guru's life, beginning with the fall of the Khalsa headquarters at Anandpur to the Mughal forces which had besieged it in alliance with the hill chieftains long hostile to him. Managing to escape from Anandpur with a few followers, the Guru was soon overwhelmed by far superior Mughal forces at Chamkaur. This became the site of a fierce engagement in which his two elder sons were killed. Under cover of darkness, however, the Guru himself was able to escape. After further pursuit, he was able some months later to find refuge in the Faridkot region of the Malwa in southern Punjab. Later tradition records that it was here, at a place called Dina, that the *Zafarnama* was written some time during the course of 1705.

The *Zafarnama* opens with a set of verses majestically invoking the omnipotence of God (verses 1–12). The letter proper begins (13–44) with backward looks at the events of December 1704, starting obliquely with a denunciation of the faithlessness of the Mughal commander whose oath falsely sworn upon the Koran caused the

Guru to abandon Anandpur (13–18). A longer section (19–44) is then devoted to a more vividly detailed evocation of the heroic struggle against far superior odds by the Sikhs at Chamkaur, culminating in the Guru's final escape.

The central part of the text (45–88) opens with the ongoing theme of outrage at the Mughal commander's betrayal of his oath (45–50). Aurangzeb himself is then at last directly addressed and reminded of the solemn undertakings on the Koran which he had made to the Guru via a messenger both orally and in writing (51–8). Further telling details are provided through the quotation of Aurangzeb's earlier instructions to the Guru, who was told first to wait at Kangar in the Malwa, then to make his way southwards by a secure route to the imperial headquarters in the Deccan where he was promised a lavishly favourable reception (59–61). Although the Guru briefly assures the emperor of his readiness to obey this summons (62–3), he then calls upon him in the name of God to practise truth and justice and to render the Guru his due (64–77). Further calling Aurangzeb to account, the Guru finally reminds him of the threat he himself continues to pose, in spite of the death of his four sons at the hands of the Mughals, and of how the small regard in which he holds the emperor and his promises is balanced only by his personal loyalty to Aurangzeb's son, Prince Muazzam (78–88).

The brief conclusion (88–111) opens with ironic praise of Aurangzeb's supposed royal virtues (88–94), which are sharply contrasted with the Guru's own earlier role as a scourge of the idol-worshipping Hindu hill chieftains (95). The poem then closes with a sententious reminder of several earlier themes, including the power of destiny and the greater power of God, of the worthlessness of worldly goods and the inability of superior physical force to subdue those who, like the Guru himself, enjoy divine favour and protection (96–111).

[Opening Invocation of God]

Eternal, gracious, wonderful,
    Kind Comforter, Deliverer,
Protector, Giver who supports,
    Sustainer who fulfils desires,
Giver of goodness, King and Guide,
    Unequalled and unparalleled,
Who needs no royal pomp and show,
    The Lord whose grace grants heaven's bliss,
5   Transcendent, mighty, manifest,
    Generous in His immanence,
Most pure and gracious Cherisher,
    Whose kindness nurtures every land,
Lord of all lands, greater than great,
    Supremely fair, kind Nourisher,
All-knowing Guardian of the weak,
    Foe-smiter who protects the poor,
Law-keeper, Prophet of the Book,
    Truth-knower, Seat of excellence,
10   Great Wisdom-seeker who knows all,
    Truth-Knower who is manifest,
Omniscient Ruler of the world,
    God solves all problems, knowing all,
And in His total knowledge makes
All actions in the world occur.

praising God

[The Loss of Anandpur]

Let God the One be witness that
    I place no trust upon this oath.
No trust at all have I in him
    Whose Bakhshis and Divans[1] speak false,
15   For those who trust Koran-sworn oaths
    Will finally be put to shame.
One whom the royal phoenix shades
    Escapes the crow's designing grasp.[2]
The lion's cover keeps him safe,
    Goats, sheep and deer are kept at bay.

Had I sworn even secretly,
     I never should have moved one step.[3]

[The Battle of Chamkaur]

But how could forty starving men
     Resist the onslaught of that horde?
They broke their oath and suddenly
     Attacked with arrows, swords and guns.
Surrounded, with no choice, in turn
     I too attacked with bow and gun.
When matters pass all other means,
     It is allowed to take up arms.
Why should I trust Koran-sworn oaths?
     What need had I to take that route?
Had I seen through his[4] foxiness,
     They'd not have made me go that way.
25   To kill or capture ill beseems
     A man who swears on the Koran.
In sudden fierce attack they rushed,
     Like swarming insects, clad in black.
One arrow drowned in blood all those
     Who dared to leave their wall's defence,
For only those who stayed behind
     Stayed safe from arrows and from shame.
When I saw Náhar[5] come to fight
     He tasted my swift arrow's point.
30   He fled, and so did many Khans
     Who'd boasted loud before the fight.
Another Afghan joined the fray,
     Swift as a flood, a shaft, a shot.
He launched repeated brave attacks,
     Some planned with care, some wildly rushed.
His onslaughts brought him many wounds,
     He killed two men,[6] then lost his life.
That cursed Khwaja dared not fight,
     But cowered back behind the wall.
35   Ah, had I seen his face, how quick
     I should have shot his sins away!

On both sides, struck by shaft and shot,
    Many fell prey to sudden death.
The arrows and the bullets rained,
    The earth was stained bright poppy-red.
The heads and limbs piled everywhere
    Seemed polo balls upon a pitch.
The world was filled with mighty noise
    From twanging bows and crackling shots.
40   The whistling of those vengeful shafts
    Made even heroes lose their wits.
But what could bravery achieve
    When forty faced that countless host?
The veiling of the world's bright lamp
    Brought forth the shining lord of night.
True keepers of Koran-sworn oaths
    Are safely guided by the Lord,
So did the Foe-Destroyer bring
    Me forth unharmed, with hair untouched.

[Address to Aurangzeb]

45   That promise-breaker[7] – I knew not –
    Was fond of lucre, false in faith,
Unrighteous and unpractising,
    For God or Prophet without care.
All those who to their faith are true
    Will keep the promises they make.
There is no trusting him, though he
    Calls on Koran and God the One.
For all his strong Koran-sworn oaths,
    I will not trust him in the least.
50   For had I trusted him at all
    I should have made my way to you.
It is your duty to observe
    That promise sworn by God to me.
If you were before me, Sire,
    Then all would be at once revealed.
It is your duty now to act
    In keeping with the words you wrote.

Your letter and your message gave
    Assurances which should be kept.
55   For promises are made to keep,
    Nor should the tongue belie the heart.
Your Kazi[8] said you'd keep your word,
    If you were true, you should have come.
Do you need that first Koran-sworn oath?
    I'll send it, and you'll see it says:
'In Kangar[9] first you may remain,
    But then the two of us should meet.
'There is no risk for you this way,
    All the Bairars[10] are ruled by me.
60   'Come and let us converse direct
    And let me show you favour too.
'Come, take a horse to suit high rank
    And rich estates besides as gifts.'
I am, my lord, your humble slave[11]
    Ready to serve at your command.
Once I receive your orders, I
    Shall readily present myself.
As you adore the One True God
    Be prompt in this affair of mine.
65   Adore Him, and do not oppress
    Any man at another's word.
Though from your throne you rule the world
    Your justice strangely suits a king.
Strange is your justice, strange – alas –
    Your faith-observance too, I fear!
How strange, how strange are your decrees!
    False promises cause only harm.
Do not have others cruelly killed –
    The sword of fate may slay you next.
70   Pay heed now, as you fear the Lord,
    Who feels no need or gratitude.
He is the fearless King of kings,
    Heaven and earth's true Sovereign,
The Lord of earth and heaven, God
    Who makes the world and all it holds.
Protecting ants and elephants,
    He smites the heedless, guards the weak.

Immune to flattery and need,
    His name is Guardian of the poor.
75   Unbending and unparalleled,
    He is the Guide who shows the way.
Be true to your Koran-sworn oath,
    Perform the promise which you made.
Let love of wisdom be your guide,
    And boldly see this matter through.
Then what if my four sons are slain?
    This coiled serpent still remains.
To put out sparks is no great deed
    Should this stir up a circling fire.
80   How well sweet-tongued Firdausi[12] said:
    'Hastiness is the devil's work.'
Be present with your witness,[13] Sire,
    Upon that day I come to you.
Do not forget, for else God will
    Most certainly forget you too,
But if you gird your loins for this,
    The Lord will grant to you His grace.
The best of acts is righteousness,
    The best of lives is knowing God.
85   These many grievous acts of yours
    Show me you do not know the Lord.
Nor does the Lord of grace know you –
    No care has He for all your wealth.
Hundreds of your Koran-sworn oaths
    Cannot inspire my slightest trust.
I'd not have come to you this way –
    The Prince's[14] call alone draws me.

[Conclusion]

Hail Aurangzeb, great king of kings,
    Fine horseman, masterly in craft,
90   Of fair appearance and bright mind,
    Great lord and master of the realm,
Skilled both in policy and war,
    Lord of the cauldron and the sword,

Brilliant in mind and fair in form,
    Divider of the empire's wealth,
Mighty in giving, firm in fight,
    Angelic, star-like majesty,
Great Aurangzeb, world-emperor –
    But like Darius[15] far from faith!

95   I was the idol-breaker when
    I slew those hill-idolaters.[16]
See how fate's faithless cycles turn
    Behind the backs of those they harm.
See too the holy power of God
    Which lets one man defeat whole hosts.
The Friend's support unarms all foes,
    For giving is the Giver's task.
He guides and grants deliverance,
    Instructing tongues in how to praise.

100   He blinds the foe before he acts
    And brings the helpless forth unhurt.
All who stay true to Him enjoy
    The mercy of the Merciful.
Those hearts which strive to serve Him best
    Obtain the shelter of the Lord.
How can his enemy deceive
    A man with whom the Guide is pleased?
Attacked by many thousands, he
    Rests safe in the Creator's care.

105   You look to armies and to gold –
    We look to thanking God who knows
Your pride in rule and wealth is matched
    By our trust in the Deathless Lord.
Since all in turn must leave, be not
    Misled in this short-stay serai.[17]
See how fate's faithless cycles turn
    Over this world and all it holds.
Use not your strength to harm the weak
    Nor chisel at your promises.

110   However many troops they lead,
    No foe harms him whom God befriends.
Nor will a thousand arts allow
    A foe to harm one hair of his.

NOTES

1 JAPJI

1 The opening phrase *sochai soch* is also taken in the older sense of the words as 'cleansing', i.e. 'Ultimate purity cannot be found in thousands of cleansings.'
2 As foreordained from the beginning.
3 The divine imperative (*hukam*), which is the basis of the natural order.
4 The ambrosial hour (*amrit vela*), when *Japji* is itself to be recited.
5 Of the human body.
6 Frequent shorthand allusion is made to places of pilgrimage (*tirath*) located by rivers as sites of ritual bathing.
7 i.e. 'by listening to the Name'. The expression in stanzas 8–11 is very condensed, with most lines beginning with *suniai*, 'through hearing', followed by a set of nouns which indicate the consequent expansion of consciousness. The wonderful sense of infinite possibilities conveyed by the packed litany (*jap*) of these stanzas is much weakened in most English versions, which prefer commentary to translation, so that these opening lines might be rendered, e.g., 'Through listening to the Name, one attains the awareness of the greatest spiritual adepts, and fathoms the mysteries of the universe.'
8 The number is regularly used as shorthand for the sixty-eight major pilgrimage sites where ritual bathing is considered especially meritorious.
9 The state of meditation is entered effortlessly, in the state called *sahaj*, 'spontaneous bliss'.
10 There is no exact English equivalent for the word used here (*manne ki*) and throughout stanzas 13–15 (*mannai*), but its sense of reverent mindfulness and remembrance is better conveyed by our 'acceptance' rather than by

the 'belief' preferred by many translators, with its inappropriate rational-istic associations.

11 A frequent expression for suffering and humiliation.

12 The mythical bull which is believed to support the earth.

13 Literally, 'rivers', taken to refer to the multiple manifestations of life.

14 Generally understood to mean that the futile effort increases the burden of sin.

15 As described above in stanzas 8–11 and 13–15.

16 Traditional Indian time-reckoning is based on the monthly cycle of lunar days (*thiti*) and the weekly cycle of solar days (*var*).

17 This stanza, called *Sodar* from its opening words *so dar*, 'that gate', is prescribed for separate daily recitation in the evening service called Sodar *Rahiras*.

18 Literally, ragas and their 'consorts' (*pari*).

19 i.e. Dharamraj, who judges the soul after death.

20 The four 'sources of life' (*khani*), created respectively from eggs, wombs, plants and sweat.

21 i.e. the order of yogis (*ai panthi*).

22 The reference in these highly condensed verses is to the making of the world as the universal mother, and to the three divine forces of creation, sustaining and destruction associated with the gods of the Hindu trinity, Brahma, Vishnu and Shiv.

23 The stanza describes the earth as the first of the five realms (*khand*), that of *dharam*, i.e. Sanskrit *dharma*, often translated as 'righteousness' or 'duty'.

24 This is the meaning generally understood for the term *saram khand*.

25 i.e. the power of the divine Name (*ram nam*). The mythological image is extended in the next line, where the beauty of those devoted to praise of the Name is compared to that of Ram's wife Sita.

26 These unnumbered verses are a *shalok*, generally attributed to the second Guru Angad, which is additional to the main sequence of the *Japji*.

2 IMPERMANENCE: THE GIFT AND CURSE OF TIME

1 In the traditional Indian time-reckoning, the night and the day were each divided into four quarters or 'watches' (*pahar*), hence the name of the poetic form (*pahare*) of this hymn, which describes life as a progress through the four watches of the night.

2 Eighty-four lakhs (literally 8,400,000) is the number given to the different kinds of existence involved in the process of transmigration.

3 With its vivid depiction of a ruling class's loss of power and wealth, this is one of the few hymns by a Guru which, unusually, has an historical associ-ation. It is one of a set, called *babarvani*, which is traditionally connected to the conquest of the Punjab from its Afghan Muslim rulers by the first Mughal emperor Babur in 1526.

4 Not realizing life's brevity and his own powerlessness, man imagines he can make something of his existence.

5 Cf. 2.1 above.
6 This hymn is composed on the pattern of the wedding songs (*ghorian*) which are addressed to the bridegroom mounted on a mare.

3 ASA KI VAR

1 The meaning is contested, and the phrase is also translated 'takes the soul with a word'.
2 Dharamraj, the Indian king of death and lord of the underworld.
3 The image is from the Indian game of ludo (*chaupar*), played with dice mentioned in the next stanza.
4 Slapping the face with a slipper was a punishment meant to humiliate as well as to hurt.

4 MIND, SELF, EGO

1 i.e. outward religious observance does not free the mind from the conditions inherent to its nature.
2 Gold is tested by being pierced with a sharp metal spike.
3 i.e. once ego is understood, the way to salvation lies open.
4 Various interpretations have been offered for this line, which is very condensed in the original. An alternative possibility is 'As You see us, so are we seen', i.e. that we are shaped by the divine view of humanity rather than by our dealings with our fellow creatures.
5 i.e. the soul or self.
6 The birds' nests are compared to dwelling in this world, their flight to the restlessness of existence.
7 The Sanskrit formula (*soham hansa*) of identity between God and the self.
8 The swallow-wort, which is as proverbial for its bitterness as the sandal is for its fragrance.
9 The moth is destroyed by its passion for the light of the candle, the deer by the sound of the musical instrument (*ghanda*) used to attract it by hunters.
10 Although not explicitly so named in this verse, it is the power of attachment to the world (*moh*) which is described in this *shalok* as the first of a set dealing with the five evil passions which also include lust or desire (*kam*), anger or wrath (*krodh*), greed or covetousness (*lobh*), and ego or pride (*ahankar*).

5 SIDDH GOSHT

1 The wooden earrings, begging wallet and patched cloak are the distinguishing marks of the Gorakhnathi yogis.
2 The Twelve Orders (*panth*) of the yogis, of which the highest advocated here is supposed to be the Ai Panth (cf. 1.28).
3 The Six Schools (*darshan*) of classical Hindu philosophy.

4 i.e. for the presence of the Word in the human heart.
5 Besides fire, earth, air and water the fifth element is ether (*akash*). Each is associated with a particular quality, respectively the power of consuming impurity, patience, coolness, impartiality and uncontaminatedness.
6 Of worldly delusion.
7 With the divine.
8 The 'total void' is the infinite divine without attributes. The 'wild goose' is, as often, an image for the soul, while the 'wall' refers to the body. The 'cave of freedom' is a technical expression used to describe the state of ultimate bliss which the practice of yoga is intended to reach.
9 Here alluding to the hardness of yogic austerity and discipline, this is a proverbial expression for an impossibly difficult task (cf. 1.37).
10 Worldly existence is believed to be governed by the three modes of being, called *sattva*, *rajas* and *tamas* in Sanskrit.
11 The eight supernatural powers (*siddhi*) which the Siddhs are believed to possess through the practice of yoga.
12 The exact meaning of the phrase (*sar apasar*) is obscure.
13 Literally, 'to have a *siddh gosht*', i.e. to enjoy the company of the saints.
14 Cf. note 2 above.
15 This formula (*nam dan isnan*) famously summarizes the Gurus' teachings on the need for devotion to the divine, for charity to others and for purity of self.
16 i.e. in the consumption of wordly delights.
17 In this stanza, the saving power of the gurmukh guided by the guru is compared to the story of the *Ramayana* telling how the island of Lanka was freed from the tyranny of the demon Ravan by Ram, aided by his brother Vibhishan.
18 The thirty-three crores (330,000,000) stand for the vast number of all living beings.
19 Of craving.
20 These questions and the answers which follow use the technical terminology of yoga, which seeks to unite the opposed energies of the 'moon' and the 'sun', located respectively in the left- and right-hand channels of the body so as to produce the state of ultimate bliss (*sahaj*).
21 i.e. the ground of the universe is selfless, not self-based.
22 The highest state of awareness.
23 The reference is to the nine apertures of the body, and to the Tenth Door which is opened at the climax of the yogic process.
24 The divine imperative (*hukam*) governing the operation of the universe.
25 The breath, when exhaled, is said to extend to a distance of ten fingers' breadths from the nostrils.
26 The contrast is between the mechanical practice of yogic austerities described here and the true mystical path described in the final lines of this stanza and in stanza 63.
27 The union of the sun with the moon is a description of the yogic process, cf. stanza 48 above.

28 i.e. the body.

29 Literally, 'there is no yoga/union' (the word *jog* has both senses).

6 ETHICAL BEING: ACTION AND GRACE

1 This second *shalok* (which also appears as *Srirag ki Var*, M1 2.1, p. 83) offers an explicit rejection of announcement of guaranteed reward for pious observance in the preceding *shalok* by Farid.

2 Literally, 'the tenth heaven', the state of bliss reached through the yogic opening of the Tenth Door.

3 The spiritual self, or the divine immanent in the soul (*atam ram*).

4 From sperm in the womb.

5 With this expression of unworthiness, the refrain underlines the condition of unregenerate humanity which is condemned to the cycle of continual rebirths in different life-forms.

6 The divine order (*hukam*), which governs existence.

7 Woman is indicated by the repeated use of the word 'vessel' (*bhand*) in this unusual *shalok*, which is regarded as a key text for the Guru's teaching on gender.

8 Literally, 'by night they are devourers of men'.

9 i.e. in the womb.

10 The Muslim name for the angel of death. In contrast to the criticism of Hindu priests in the preceding pieces, this hymn draws on the Muslim conception of the afterlife.

7 ANAND SAHIB

1 Literally, 'with spontaneity' (*sahaj seti*), i.e. without any self-willed effort.

2 The ragas are the main musical modes, and their 'consorts' (*paria*) are understood to be the subsidiary raginis which are associated with them.

3 A wonderful description of the bliss experienced by the heart filled with the divine presence. The 'heavenly music', literally, a mixture of all five kinds of sounds (*panch-shabad*), is like the 'music that's silent' (*anhad*) in the last line of the stanza.

4 An image (*kal kantak*) of death's power to wound and to terrify.

5 The real love evoked by the divine.

6 i.e. the bhaktas (*bhagat*), whose narrower sense of 'pre-Nanak saints' whose works are included in the Guru Granth Sahib is perhaps alluded to in the phrase 'more sharp than a sword and more fine than a hair', used by Farid to describe the narrow bridge to salvation which the Muslim soul must traverse after death.

7 'Balance' is used here to translate *sahaj* 'spontaneity, harmonious existence' (see Introduction). What the word *sahaj* refers to is the middle path between self and non-self, existence and non-existence, action and non-action, death and life, etc. It is a 'standpoint' that is opposed to such dualities, which arise only from the standpoint of the self.

8 The evil spirits (*betal*) who take possession of dead bodies.

9 The sense of this stanza suggests the translation of *bani*, literally 'Word', as a hymn of the guru (*gurbani*), as in stanzas 24 and 27 below. But the more generalized spiritual sense of 'Word' seems appropriate in stanza 25.

10 i.e. all creation is subject to the divinely instituted natural order (*hukam*).

11 i.e. the ground of action and its awareness is the same divine principle.

12 The three modes (*gun*) which make up the frame of everyday thinking: space, time and causality (cf. 5.20)

13 The snare of the seemingly real delights of this world (*maya*).

14 i.e. in the body.

8 GURU AS WORD: THE LOCATION OF AUTHORITY

1 These verses vividly describe how touring troupes of actor-dancers perform plays on mythological themes.

2 The exclamation of general approval, *vahu vahu*, indicates the later Sikh use of Vahiguru (Waheguru) 'How Wonderful is the Guru!' as a title for the divine.

3 The word here (*karam*) is also taken to mean 'by good deeds'.

4 The capital is used, since these verses refer to the practices enjoined upon the early Sikh community by the living Guru.

5 The 'pool filled with nectar' (*amritsar*) is the Name.

6 Or 'reciting *Japji*'.

7 These verses are inspired by the poetic theme of the joys of the Indian rainy season, when nature is renewed in such spectacular fashion.

9 SHABAD HAZARE (PATSHAHI 10)

1 See the Glossary of Names for these titles of Vishnu.

2 i.e. Krishna, as described in the *Bhagavadgita*.

3 See the Glossary of Names for these sages.

4 The classic Sanskrit formula *neti neti* which denies the possibility of defining the divine, literally, 'it's not so, it's not so'.

5 The standard pair of Hindu and Muslim names for God.

6 The World-Snake (*Sheshnag*) which supports the world.

7 'Dark' (*shyam*) is the epithet of Krishna.

10 COMMUNICATING ECSTASY: KNOWLEDGE AND NON-KNOWLEDGE

1 i.e. the holy books recited by the orthodox Brahmins who are the target of these verses.

2 The pose of the crane as it stands on one leg on the river bank while on the look-out for fish is a common symbol of hypocritical piety.

3 Indian brides move permanently to their in-laws after marriage, so this expression (*sasurai peiai*) stands for 'in life and after death'. This *shalok* also appears in the Adi Granth (p. 1378) as Shalok Farid 32.

4 Red is the colour worn by Indian brides.

5 i.e. the look (*nadar*) of divine favour.

6 Since it refers to the identity of the Absolute, the word *ape* has here been translated 'the Same One', which is more appropriate than the objectification of the divine identity which is risked in the sometimes unavoidable renderings as e.g. 'He Himself' adopted elsewhere.

7 The slime in the net represents the created delusion of worldly goods.

8 Spelt *ngian* in this acrostic poem, the same as *gian* elsewhere, usually translated as 'wisdom'.

9 In these verses, the word *akhar* 'letter' is variously interpreted by the commentaries, but it may most easily be understood as having the sense throughout of 'one letter (*akhar*) of the Name', representing the smallest conceivable unit of divine power.

10 While the primary sense is 'in the mind', these verses also mark the closure of the Adi Granth, implying the parallel sense of 'in the scripture'.

11 ZAFARNAMA

1 The senior military and civil officers of the Mughal state.

2 This and the next verse allude to the divine protection which preserved the Guru from the false promises of Aurangzeb's officers.

3 i.e. in withdrawing from Anandpur.

4 Referring to the Bakhshi in command of the Mughal forces at Chamkaur.

5 Nahar Khan of Maler, an Afghan officer in the Mughal army.

6 Identified by some commentators as the Guru's two sons who fell at Chamkaur.

7 i.e. the Mughal commander.

8 Aurangzeb's earlier messenger.

9 A village in the Faridkot region in southern Panjab.

10 The Rajput tribe controlling the southward route which the Guru would have to take from Kangar to the imperial headquarters in the Deccan.

11 The tone of this verse is heavily ironical.

12 The great Persian poet whose classic epic the *Shahnama* or *Book of Kings* provides the formal model for the *Zafarnama*.

13 Taken to refer to the Kazi who had been Aurangzeb's early messenger (see note 8).

14 The Guru was on friendly terms with Aurangzeb's son Prince Muazzam, later Bahadur Shah I.

15 The unrighteous Persian emperor defeated and slain by Alexander the Great.

16 The Hindu hill chieftains who were allied with the Mughals against the Guru.

17 i.e. the world.

GLOSSARY OF NAMES

The system used in this book for spelling Indian names is a compromise between their classical Sanskrit forms and the sometimes considerably different Gurmukhi spellings of the Sikh scriptures. Since the Sanskrit forms are likely to be most familiar to Western readers, we have generally favoured these, but have usually dropped the final short -*a* which is omitted in Punjabi and most modern Indian languages. In the list of names given below, the full Sanskrit forms in brackets are marked with accents to show the long vowels, as a guide to pronunciation. The few Arabic and Persian names used by the Gurus are similarly included in the list.

Arjun (Sk. *Arjuna*), the charioteer of Krishna in the *Bhagavadgita*.
Aurangzeb (Pers.), Mughal emperor (r. 1658–1707).
Azrael (Ar. *Azrāīl*), Islamic name of the angel of death.
Babur (Pers. Bābur), Mughal emperor (r. 1526–30).
Bairar (*Bairār*), name of a Rajput tribe.
Bakhshi (Pers. *Bakhshī*), Mughal title of a senior military officer.
Brahma (Sk. *Brahman-*, *Brahmā*), the Hindu god of creation.
Buddha (Sk.), Buddha, sage.
Charpat, name of a great yogi.
Chitra Gupta (Sk.), the scribes of death who record man's deeds.
Darius (Pers. *Dārā*), the Persian emperor Darius III (r. 336–330 BCE).
Devaki (Sk. *Devakī*), mother of Krishna.
Dharam (Sk. *Dharma*), the god of death and judgement.
Dhruv (Sk. *Dhruva*), name of a great sage.
Divan (Pers. *Dīvān*), Mughal title of a senior civil official.
Firdausi (Pers. *Firdausī*), Persian epic poet.
Gopi (Sk. *Gopī*), milkmaid companion of Krishna.

Gorakh (Sk. *Goraksha*), name of a great yogi.
Govind (Sk. *Govinda*), a title of Krishna.
Indra (Sk.), the Hindu god of the sky.
Ishvar (Sk. *Īshvara*), a title of Shiv.
Kangar (*Kāngar*), name of a village.
Kazi (Ar.Pers. *Qāzī*), Muslim judge.
Khan (Pers. *Khān*), Afghan title.
Khwaja (Pers. *Khwāja*), Muslim title.
Koran (Ar. *Qur'ān*), the Muslim scripture.
Krishna (Sk.), the eighth incarnation of Vishnu.
Lanka (Sk. *Lankā*), the island kingdom of Ravan, conquered by Ram.
Loharipa (*Lohārīpā*), name of a great yogi.
Madh (Sk. *Madhu*), a demon slain by Krishna.
Madhav (Sk. *Mādhava*), a title of Krishna.
Mahesh (Sk. *Mahesha*), a title of Shiv.
Meru (Sk.), the mythic Mount Meru in the Himalayas.
Mukand (Sk. *Mukunda*), a title of Vishnu.
Murar (Sk. *Murāri*), a title of Krishna.
Nahar (*Nāhar*), name of an Afghan officer.
Nand (Sk. *Nanda*), foster-father of Krishna.
Narad (Sk. *Nārada*), name of a sage.
Nath (Sk. *Nātha*), 'Lord', title given to yogic masters.
Parasar (Sk. *Parāshara*), name of a sage.
Parvati (Sk. *Pārvatī*), the divine consort of Shiv.
Pir (Pers. *Pīr*), title of Sufi elder.
Purana (Sk. *Purāna*), most recent category of Hindu scripture.
Rahim (Ar. *Rahīm*), the Merciful, title of Allah.
Ram (Sk. *Rāma*), the seventh incarnation of Vishnu, hero of the *Ramayana*.
Ramachandra (Sk. *Rāmachandra*), title of Ram.
Ravan (Sk. *Rāvana*), demon king of Lanka, slain by Ram.
Shastra (Sk. *Shāstra*), Hindu law book.
Shaykh (Ar. *Shaykh*), title of Muslim religious leader.
Shiv (Sk. *Shiva*), great Hindu god.
Siddh (Sk. *Siddha*), sage, great yogic master.
Sita (Sk. *Sītā*), wife of Ram.
Smriti (Sk.), post-Vedic Hindu scripture.
Veda (Sk.), the most ancient category of Hindu scripture.
Vibhishan (Sk. *Vibhīshana*), younger brother of Ram.
Vishnu (Sk.), great Hindu god, incarnated as Ram and as Krishna.
Vyas (Sk. *Vyāsa*), great Hindu sage, believed to have arranged the Vedas.
Yasodha (Sk. *Yashodhā*), foster-mother of Krishna.

BIBLIOGRAPHY

The suggestions for further reading contained in the following pages are broadly arranged to follow the sequence of topics discussed in the Introduction. The coverage of topics in the secondary literature is very uneven, and for some there are as yet no studies worth recommending. Except for editions of the scriptural texts on which our translations are based, only significant titles written in English have been included.

The best general introduction to the history and institutions of the religion is W. H. McLeod, *Sikhism*, London: Penguin, 1998. This contains its own very helpful bibliography covering a much wider range of subjects than is addressed here. The history is covered in J. S. Grewal, *The Sikhs of the Punjab*, 2nd edn, Cambridge: Cambridge University Press, 1998, again with an ample bibliographic essay. A great deal of information on individual topics is conveniently accessible in the four volumes of Harbans Singh (ed.), *The Encyclopaedia of Sikhism*, Patiala: Punjabi University, 1992–8, whose articles are accompanied by short bibliographies of relevant English and Punjabi titles. Finally, a broad overview of the emphases of contemporary Sikh studies in the West may be gained from the introduction and contents of C. Shackle, Gurharpal Singh and A. S. Mandair (eds), *Sikh Religion, Culture and Ethnicity*, Richmond: Curzon, 2001.

Any list of studies of the Sikh Gurus must again begin with a work by the highly productive and influential New Zealand scholar W. H. McLeod, *Guru Nanak and the Sikh Religion*, Oxford: Clarendon Press, 1968, which may be supplemented by the same author's more detailed study of the hagiographic traditions, *Early Sikh Tradition: A Study of the Janamsakhis*, Oxford: Clarendon Press, 1980. For Guru Gobind Singh, the best account is J. S. Grewal and S. S. Bal, *Guru Gobind Singh: A Biographical Study*, 2nd edn, Chandigarh: Panjab University, 1987.

A very clear summary account of the organization of the Adi Granth and of the traditionally acknowledged early recensions of the text is to be found in the essay on 'The Sikh scriptures', included in W. H. McLeod, *The Evolution of the Sikh Community: Five Essays*, Oxford: Clarendon Press, 1976, pp. 59–82. More recently, the formation of the scriptural canon has been looked at by G. S. Mann, first in *The Goindval Pothis: The Earliest Extant Source of the Sikh Canon*, Cambridge, Mass.: Department of Sanskrit and Indian Studies, Harvard University, 1996, then in *The Making of Sikh Scripture*, New York: Oxford University Press, 2001. Another recent approach is presented in Pashaura Singh, *The Guru Granth Sahib: Canon, Meaning and Authority*, New Delhi: Oxford University Press, 2000, while key issues are critically addressed in the important article by J. S. Deol, 'Text and lineage in early Sikh history: issues in the study of the Adi Granth', *Bulletin of the School of Oriental and African Studies (BSOAS)* 64 (2001), pp. 34–58.

The Dasam Granth has yet to receive comparable scholarly attention, but a useful introduction to its contents is provided in C. H. Loehlin, *The Granth of Guru Gobind Singh and the Khalsa Brotherhood*, Lucknow: Lucknow Publishing House, 1971, while numerous references to its historical position will be found in W. H. McLeod, *Sikhs of the Khalsa: A History of the Khalsa Rahit*, New Delhi: Oxford University Press, 2003.

Those who want to be able to approach the Adi Granth in its original language are directed to C. Shackle, *An Introduction to the Sacred Language of the Sikhs*, London: SOAS, 1983, to be supplemented by his *A Guru Nanak Glossary*, 2nd edn, New Delhi: Heritage, 1995. Studies of the linguistic varieties used by the Gurus and of their stylistic implications are presented in C. Shackle, 'Approaches to the Persian loans in the Adi Granth', *BSOAS* 41 (1977), pp. 73–96; 'The Sahaskriti poetic idiom in the Adi Granth', *BSOAS* 41 (1978), pp. 297–313; and 'The South-Western style in the Guru Granth Sahib', *Journal of Sikh Studies* 5 (1978), pp. 137–60.

The broader Hindi literary context is described in R. S. McGregor, *Hindi Literature from its Beginnings to the Nineteenth Century*, Wiesbaden: Harrassowitz, 1984. This context also informs the study of one of the Bhagats included in the Adi Granth presented in W. M. Callewaert and P. G. Friedlander, *The Life and Works of Raidas*, New Delhi: Manohar, 1992. R. Snell, *The Hindi Classical Tradition: A Braj Bhasa Reader*, London: SOAS, 1991, provides a particularly useful introduction to the main features of classical Hindi poetry, with extensive translations and select bibliography.

Turning to the Sikh scriptures themselves, the pioneering official English version of the colonial period was published 'by order of the Secretary of State for India in Council' as E. Trumpp (trans.), *The Adi Granth or the Holy Scriptures of the Sikhs*, London: Allen, Trubner, 1877. M. A. Macauliffe, *The Sikh Religion: Its Gurus, Sacred Writings and Authors*, 6 vols in 3, Oxford: Clarendon Press, 1909, reprinted New Delhi: S. Chand, 1963, has never really been superseded. It remains of considerable value for its combination of extensive translations of the Gurus' hymns with traditional accounts of their lives, particularly in view of the rather surprising continuing absence in the English secondary literature of first-class studies of many of the Gurus.

The critique of the neo-colonial reformulation of the teachings of the Sikh Gurus by the Singh Sabha reformists has been a central concern of A. S. Mandair for a number of years. The general issues involved are explored at length in his monograph *Religion and the Politics of Translation*, Manchester: Manchester University Press (forthcoming 2006). Closer studies of this phenomenon include his articles 'The work of transcendence in modern Sikh theology', to appear in *Journal of the American Academy of Religions* 73 (2006), and 'The emergence of "Sikh Theology": Reassessing the passage of ideas from Trumpp to Bhai Vir Singh', *BSOAS* 68 (2005), which looks at the implications of the monotheistic interpretation of the opening formulae of the Adi Granth by the great Singh Sabha exegete Bhai Vir Singh.

Of the several complete translations of the Adi Granth into English which have appeared since the 1960s, particular mention may be made of the useful prose version with superscript numbers indicating word-for-word correspondences with the original provided in Manmohan Singh (trans.), *Sri Guru Granth Sahib*, 8 vols, Amritsar: Shiromani Gurdwara Parbandhak Committee (SGPC), 1969. The increasing quantity of material available electronically includes S. S. Khalsa (trans.), *Sri Guru Granth Sahib: Khalsa Consensus Translation*, at www.sikhs.org.

A summary overview of the strategies typically adopted in the translation of the Sikh scriptures, with a fairly full bibliography, is included in C. Shackle, 'From gentlemen's outfitters to hyperbazaar: a personal approach to translating the sacred', in L. Long (ed.), *Translation and Religion: Holy Untranslatable?*, Clevedon: Multilingual Matters, 2005. Only some of the many English translations of selections from the Sikh Gurus can be mentioned here. The versions presented in Khushwant Singh (trans.), *Hymns of Guru Nanak*, New Delhi: Orient Longmans, 1969, reflect the key role this writer had played in producing the translations included in Trilochan Singh et al. (trans.), *Selections from the Sacred Writings of the Sikhs*, London: Allen & Unwin, 1960. A very useful selection with explanatory material, albeit produced in a very crabbed format, will be found in W. H. McLeod (ed. and trans.), *Textual Sources for the Study of Sikhism*, Manchester: Manchester University Press, 1984. More attractively produced versions, including a complete translation of the *Sukhmani* by Guru Arjan, are presented in Nikky Guninder-Kaur Singh (trans.), *The Name of my Beloved: Verses of the Sikh Gurus*, San Francisco: HarperCollins, 1995, whose translation strategy reflects the feminist perspective of her monograph *The Feminine Principle in the Sikh Vision of the Transcendent*, Cambridge: Cambridge University Press, 1993.

Besides translations from the Sikh Gurus, attention may be drawn here to the existence of several translations of the works of the Bhagats also included in the Adi Granth, notably the two volumes produced by N. Dass (trans.), *Songs of Kabir from the Adi Granth*, Albany: State University of New York Press, 1991, and *Songs of the Saints from the Adi Granth*, Albany: State University of New

York Press, 2000. Pashaura Singh, *The Bhagats of the Guru Granth Sahib: Sikh Self-Definition and the Bhagat-Bani*, New Delhi: Oxford University Press, 2003, provides a recent overview of the Sikh understanding of the position of the Bhagats in the scripture.

As in every other respect, in terms of translation too the Dasam Granth has been much less well served than the Adi Granth. Besides the relevant volume of Macauliffe's *Sikh Religion*, selections are included in S. S. Sekhon (trans.), *Unique Drama: Translation of Benati Chaupai, Bachitra Natak and Akal Ustati*, Chandigarh: Guru Gobind Singh Foundation, 1968, and in Gopal Singh (trans.), *Thus Spake the Tenth Master*, Patiala: Punjabi University, 1978. The first volumes have now appeared of an intended complete prose translation, Jodh Singh and Dharam Singh (trans.), *Sri Dasam Granth Sahib: Text and Translation*, Patiala: Heritage Publications, 1999–.

While we have learnt much from the many translators who have preceded us, we must however conclude by acknowledging our primary debt, which is to several fine commentaries produced in modern Punjabi. For the Adi Granth these notably include the *Shabadarath Sri Guru Granth Sahib ji*, 4 vols, Amritsar: SGPC, 1959–69, and Sahib Singh (ed.), *Sri Guru Granth Sahib Darpan*, 10 vols, Jullundur: Raj Publishers, 1962–4, besides the edition of Guru Nanak's works in Taran Singh (ed.), *Guru Nanak Bani Prakash*, 2 vols, Patiala: Punjabi University, 1969. The Dasam Granth, too, is better served in terms of recent Punjabi scholarship than it is in English, particularly in Randhir Singh (ed.), *Shabadarath Dasam Granth Sahib*, 3 vols, Patiala: Punjabi University, 1995, and in R. S. Jaggi and G. K. Jaggi (eds), *Sri Dasam-Granth Sahib: Path-Sampadan ate Viakhia*, 5 vols, New Delhi: Gobind Sadan, 1999.

INDEX

Related titles from Routledge

Religions of South Asia
Edited by Sushil Mittal and Gene R. Thursby

South Asia is home to many of the world's most vibrant religious faiths. It is also one of the most dynamic and historically rich regions on earth, where changing political and social structures have caused religions to interact and hybridise in unique ways. This textbook introduces the contemporary religions of South Asia, from the indigenous religions such as the Hindu, Jain, Buddhist and Sikh traditions, to incoming influences such as Christianity, Judaism and Islam. In ten chapters, it surveys the nine leading belief systems of South Asia and explains their history, practices, values and worldviews. A final chapter helps students relate what they have learnt to religious theory, paving the way for future study.

Entirely written by leading experts, *Religions of South Asia* combines solid scholarship with clear and lively writing to provide students with an accessible and comprehensive introduction. All chapters are specially designed to aid cross-religious comparison, following a standard format covering set topics and issues; the book reveals to students the core principles of each faith, compares it to neighbouring traditions, and its particular place in South Asian history and society. It is a perfect resource for all students of South Asia's diverse and fascinating faiths.

Hb: 0-415-22390-3
Pb: 0-415-22391-1

Available at all good bookshops
For ordering and further information please visit:
www.routledges.com

Related titles from Routledge

Religion: The Basics
Maloroy Nye

How does religion fit in with life in the modern world? Do you have to 'believe' to be a part of one?

From televangelism in the American South to the wearing of the hijab in Britain and Egypt; from the rise of paganism to the aftermath of 9/11, this accessible guide looks at the ways in which religion interacts with the everyday world in which we live. It is a comprehensive introduction to the world of religion, and covers aspects including:

• Religion and culture
• How power operates in religion
• Gender issues
• The role of belief, rituals and religious texts
• Religion in the contemporary world

Religion: The Basics offers an invaluable and up-to-date overview for anyone wanting to find out more about this fascinating subject.

'Finally, a book written for the general reader that communicates clearly and authoritatively the many advances that have taken place in the academic study of religion over the past generation.'
Russell T McCutcheon, University of Alabama

0-415-26379-4

Available at all good bookshops
For ordering and further information please visit:
www.routledges.com